Uranus Is Always Funny

Short Essays to Make You Laugh

Uranus Is Always Funny

Short Essays to Make You Laugh

Bill Spencer

Cover illustration by Eli Connaughton Jordan

Cover design by Dwayne Booth. Book design by
HumorOutcasts Press.

Author photo by Carolyn Elkins

Published 2020 by HumorOutcasts Press
Printed in the United States of America

ISBN: 978-0-9600085-7-5

for

Carolyn

ACKNOWLEDGEMENTS

Profuse, heartfelt thanks to the editors of the publications/places where some of these essays previously appeared: *Funny Times*, *The Sun*, HumorOutcasts.com, *Clever* magazine, *The Inconsequential*, *Hobo Pancakes*, The Short Humour Site, and *Nuthouse*. I especially wish eternal blessings upon Sandee Beyerle and Donna Cavanagh for their friendship and support. May flowers spring up in their footsteps and bloom forever. I'm also indebted more than I can say to Judi Hill and the entire Wildacres Writers Workshop community. They changed my life.

Special thanks to the Blumenthal family for generously providing Wildacres Retreat for the betterment of human relations. Many of these essays were written there, one of my favorite places on Earth.

I'm endlessly grateful to my wife, Carolyn Elkins, for her support, encouragement, and expert editing. Whatever missteps are in these essays, she almost certainly advised me against. And I hereby publicly admit—this isn't easy for me—that she is even funnier than I am.

CONTENTS

STUDENT BLOOPERS 195

Who the Hell Am I?

Baby, I Was Born to Pun

I'm a humorist. But it's not my fault. It wasn't a choice. I was born that way.

People have exhorted me for years to tell my story. "You oughta write about it," they said. "You oughta publish your biography." So here it is: a brief oughta-biography of my life as a humoro-textual. Let me say up front that at this point—through the gifts of energy, enthusiasm, and stamina—I have laughed with literally hundreds of women. (Men, too, but that's a subject for another essay.) I've been a virtual Casanova of comedy. But how did I get here?

As incredible as it sounds, my parents recognized my inclination and "talent" from the moment I was born. According to family stories, my mother's first words after she took me in her arms were "He smells funny." So you can see that even from the very beginning I was developing my scents of humor.

Later in life, even complete strangers could tell what I was. When I was very young and my family traveled from our home in Georgia to upstate New York, the neighborhood kids noticed my humor expertise right away. "You talk funny," they all said.

While it's a living hell for some, I think I may have actually peaked in high school. It was a time of almost constant reinforcement of my sense of comic self. Teachers repeatedly reassured me, "You have a very funny effect on everyone around you." And from my classmates, the compliments just kept rolling in: "You dress funny. You dance funny. You even *look* funny." My school counselor also jumped on the bandwagon. I can't tell you how much it meant to me to have a highly educated professional unreservedly praising me—before I'd had any formal training even—as "absolutely hysterical." He also encouraged me to hire an agent to help advance me in the career I was clearly destined for by persistently urging me to "get help." I was so grateful for this support.

As a young man, I took my secret superpower into the bar scene, where I exploited it—perhaps unfairly—in flirtations with women. I dazzled them with my wit: "If I said you had a beautiful body, would you hold it against me?" Many of these young ladies were so tickled that they actually enunciated the words "Ha, Ha," and most indicated their appreciation of my originality. "I've never heard *that* one before," they admitted. Some—quite a few actually— would pay me compliments that I treasure to this day. Often something along the lines of "You're a regular laugh riot, aren't you?" I was impressed they could tell so much about me from just my opening line.

With all this lifelong encouragement to a career in comedy, it's no wonder I became a humor writer. I'd like to express my gratitude for the kind, heartening praise I received from several editors, who convinced me, despite my doubts, that my writing was indeed "laughable."

Some people have a head for business. I have a head for making people laugh little laughs. Thanks to all of you who've acknowledged this. The coveted epithet you bestowed on me is my favorite compliment. Because of you, I realize that perhaps—just perhaps—I've *earned* your oft-repeated description of me as "chuckle-headed."

I had to work hard for every giggle in my earlier days, so please forgive me if I enjoy the ease of my profession now. Now that I'm in my 60's, most days I even *feel* funny. It's very gratifying and pleasurable to rest on one's laurels. I thank my lucky stars that I've reached a zenith where all I have to do now is say to anyone who knows me, "I'm a humorist," and they laugh.

They laugh their heads off.

Being Ricardo Montalban

A funny thing about our personal identity is that although we work so hard and long to find it, we often delight in hiding or abandoning it. Who hasn't had fun wearing a costume, assuming a persona, or acting a role in a play or skit?

For 25 years I've attended a writers' workshop that requires everyone to wear a name tag at all times. This is indisputably a wise policy, and I've always followed it. Actually, I've always followed the letter of this law, but there was one year that I may have skirted its spirit. That particular year some devil-possessed troublemaker suggested an exchange of name tags. Two people traded tags, then two others, and it snowballed until about half the writers were wearing name tags not their own. During the next few days I saw 5 or 6 different Bill Spencers, including women, go by. At some meals I sat across the table from Bill Spencer. Once I remember hearing a lot of laughing at another table and looked over to see that Bill Spencer was having a lot more fun than I was.

When a frustrated newcomer complained to the workshop director, she responded, "They're writers. What do you expect?" We *were* wearing name tags at all times, and since the trades were freely made, the tags were technically "our" name tags even if they didn't have our names on them. You may be wondering who started this trouble, and I wish I could tell you, but this was years ago, and he of course was wearing someone else's name tag.

So when I instigated this experiment in identity fluidity, it was all because I envied one of the most admired teachers at the workshop. I'll call him Brad Pitt. I proposed a tag exchange with this faculty star and was stunned when he agreed. I was thrilled. I had definitely traded up. I was a lowly non-writing spouse, and he was a supremely talented creative writer, a masterful teacher, an amazing musician, and a legend with the ladies. Who WOULDN'T want to be Brad Pitt?

As it turned out, *I* wouldn't. . . . I happily, even giddily wore Brad's name tag for more than 2 days—but on the third day—and I'm as surprised as you are that I'm saying this—I began to want my own name tag back—my own name tag with my own name.

Though I don't fully understand why this was, I believe my dubious acting "career" has given me at least some insight into my longing. The fourth year that I attended this same workshop, the director—a woman you do not say no to—came to my room and asked, "Do you think you could do Ricardo Montalban?" When I asked for a little more context, she said she'd written a skit for an end-of-the-week show, a parody of *Fantasy Island*, and she was considering casting me as Mr. Roarke. I told her I'd try my best to "do" Ricardo. This led to my performing Mr. Roarke no fewer than 10 times over the next 15 years. I do confess I liked being Ricardo. I wore a white dinner jacket, slicked back my hair, said my lines with a Spanish accent, and walked and stood with a limp. (Yes, I did say "*stood* with a limp.") Often after these performances I would be asked to again say, "Tattoo" or "Cordoba," and more than a few people advised me to *always* wear my hair slicked back. It was made pretty clear to me that as Ricardo Montalban I was more interesting, better-looking, and certainly more sexually attractive than Bill Spencer ever was.

However, despite this compelling incentive, I could never manage to stay in Ricardo's character more than about an hour. Sure, he was suave, intriguing, and alluring—but he cost me way too much effort. I had to keep my chest painfully puffed out, had to maintain impeccable posture, and had to be debonair at all times. You know what? Being someone other than ourselves is damn hard.

My acting brought home to me that we are who we are because that's who we're most comfortable being.

Being anyone else is just too tiring.

Role Model in Reverse

Back when I was a young, naive lad of 35, I embraced as my role model an author famed for his language-humor columns and books. He was doing what I loved—punning and word-playing—and, amazingly, he was making a living at it. So I was thrilled when I learned he was coming to speak at the university where I taught. I was going to get to hobnob with my ideal self.

Before I actually met him, I heard he had asked one of my colleagues, the visit's sponsor, to launder his underwear for him. This was unsettling. I had associated him with a superhero's cape—not skivvies. Suddenly, Super Punster seemed more like Captain Underpants. You might say he lost some of my respect—but only briefly.

He regained some stature when he offered to speak to individual classes and I was able to schedule him to address my own English 101 students. What a treat this would be. He arrived at my classroom with an armload of his own books and immediately began propping them up against the blackboard at the front of the room. I had expected he would make a presentation both entertaining and educational. But what he actually did was go down the row of his displayed books in a long sales pitch about why my students should buy each one. He concluded with a long story about a relative who experienced some trouble, and I was sympathizing until he ended with a punchline. I had thought he was confiding a personal experience to us, but it turned out to be just a long setup for a pun. I don't remember the exact shtick, but it was akin to the one that ends, "Pardon me, Roy, is that the cat who chewed your new shoes?"

At dinner later that day, he again hit us with the same shtick, and at his auditorium reading that night he told for the *third* time Uncle Roy's sneaker-snacking cat tale. I began to doubt the spontaneity of my hero's wit.

After the auditorium presentation, I stood in line to get two new books inscribed. Maybe my role model wasn't the all-around ideal I had hoped for, but I was still impressed by his success. He sat at a table on the stage just like other visiting authors before him. What was different was that he had brought his own huge, badly wrinkled author's banner with him and had taped it to the front of the table. He was unmistakably open for business. When I was second in line, I heard his conversation with the woman in front of me. She was a high school teacher, and I could see that she had just bought two of his books. His "conversation" consisted of touting the merits of other books of his that she really ought to also buy. "Was this cool?" I wondered, but I congratulated myself that at least I would be immune to his hard sell since the two books I was buying would give me the complete collection. I mentioned that fact immediately to stave off the sales pressure, but he surprised me: "I'll make you a special price," he said, "if you require your students to buy my books for your classes." This is when it dawned on me, "Oh, *this* is how you make a living at wordplay."

In his novel *Cat's Cradle*, Kurt Vonnegut invents the very useful term "wrang-wrang," which he defines as a reverse role model, someone who represents the ridiculous extreme of a path you yourself are on. What made me so uneasy about my idol's self-promotion and his repeated shaggy dog cat story is that I myself had been accused of frequently interjecting puns into conversations with my friends. I felt I was honing my craft. Nevertheless, some complained that I didn't listen with genuine concern but rather with an ear to how I might display my too-ready wit. Perhaps they told me about how their students were in open revolt and I had said, "Sounds like you've lost your class." Maybe I wasn't at the end of the path, but I was on it.

As my wife and friends will tell you, even after I met my wrang-wrang, I still interject the occasional pun. But I think I've grown. These days if you told me your pet rat had died from eating varnish, I definitely would *not* say, "That was a terrible end, a horrible end—but a beautiful finish."

World's Biggest Fan

I've been in love with the same woman for 45 years. Please don't tell my wife.

Actually, my wife knows.

At the age of 15, I remember being mystified by classmates who acted gaga over particular celebrities. Then I heard Olivia Newton-John sing. I've never been mellow since.

In 1973 I was delivering *The Daily Sun* when "Let Me Be There" started playing on my bicycle-handlebar-mounted transistor radio. (Yes, there were such things, and I had one.) Despite the limitations of my sound equipment, I don't think I've ever heard anything more wonderful. I was enraptured. I was gone. And I had an epiphany: "Oh, *this* is what it feels like to be a fan. This is what it feels like to be hopelessly devoted to a doomed-to-be-unrequited love."

Now, from a decades-later perspective, I've learned the wisdom that one should never start anything that could be considered a "collection." But at 15, I was not wise. The next day I bought my first Olivia Newton-John 45 record and began a collection that now includes 15 vinyl albums, 4 cassette tapes (in a box under the house), 9 CDs, a Betamax recording of *Two of a Kind*, 4 VHS videos and films, 3 DVD videos and films, 4 oversized concert programs, a sheet music book, a box full of newspaper and magazine clippings, 2 T-shirts (one with an iron-on image of Olivia), an empty plastic bag from Koala Blue (Olivia's short-lived clothing store), and a whole folder of materials exclusively for members of her official fan club. (Yes, there was such a thing, and I joined it.) I also used to have several beautiful wall posters but lost them in a leaky-ceiling accident, and I once had several 45s but ruined them during a termite-situation panic. (Don't ask.)

Some of my teen friends also fell for Olivia but not as early as I did. I considered them Olivia Newton-Johnny-come-lately's. We all went to see her live in concert in Atlanta, but our seats were about a hundred rows back. Though we saw her, she didn't see us, which only intensified our pangs.

So we hatched a brilliant plan. More of a fantasy than a plan, really, but it gave us a kind of hope. Four of us would go out to Malibu, where Olivia had a house, and hang around on the beach as long as it took for us to casually encounter her. One of us would act as the villain and accost her in some obnoxious manner, perhaps by yelling at her, "Hey, Olivia, let's get physical" or "Let me hear your body talk." At this point the other three of us would show up and rescue the songstress in distress by giving our cohort the drubbing of his life. Olivia, then, would of course invite her heroes back to her place. The only thing that stood between me and unimaginable bliss was Tim's, Mike's, and Bobby's unwillingness to take on the beaten-to-a-pulp bad guy role. The selfish bastards.

I've been to five of Olivia's concerts, the last one a few years ago. The expensive ticket was a gift from a good friend who knows of my continuing soft spot for a certain saucy Aussie with a still-angelic voice. At the concert Olivia asked us to stand if we'd ever seen *Grease*, and I leapt to my feet. She asked us to remain standing if we'd seen it more than ten times, and I had to sit down. At the end, one man remained standing, claiming he'd seen the movie "more than a hundred times." The bastard.

I saw a photo of Olivia and John Travolta in *People* magazine a few weeks ago. They were celebrating a 40-year *Grease* retrospective, and, I admit, I didn't cut the photo out. In fact, I haven't cut any clippings in years. I realize it's barely possible that I'm not Olivia's absolutely biggest fan in the world ever.

But in case you're reading this, Olivia, I don't want to miss this chance to say—I love you. I honestly love you.

The VW Bug and Rocket Science

In 1972, the same year that the final Apollo mission flew, I found myself without a ride to high school. Yes, we could get to the moon, but could I get to school?

I lived about a 30-minute drive from the Catholic high school I attended (Mount de Sales), and my sophomore year I and my brother John, who also attended MDS, had lost our previous year's transportation. So I got right on the phone to work the problem. Well, I wish I could say that. Actually, it was my mother who got on the phone. She determined that our best shot was getting a ride with Mr. C, who taught at Mount de Sales and who lived only about a mile away. But Mr. C said no. He said he'd had riders before and they were interrupters of morning routine, always getting in the way and causing delays. After his last experience he'd sworn off all riders forever. When my mother's efforts following other leads all failed, we finally had to face the inescapable gravity of the situation. Desperate, my mother called Mr. C back and begged him to reconsider. She offered to pay him generously and assured him we'd be no trouble: he'd never even see us; we would just wait in the car. Under these terms, Mr C relented.

Now, what all this effort, bribing, and pleading got us was a 1960s Volkswagen Beetle. Picture a cute, shiny, colorful VW Bug. Mr. C's car was nothing like that. His Bug was old, a dull gray—or at least it had been gray at some point. And these subcompacts are awfully small inside—with only about the same interior space as an Apollo command module, a tight fit for 3 men. Mr. C had two children also going to MDS, so that meant 5 of us had to fit into the Bug. Mr. C and his son sat up front, and his daughter (whom I'll call Betty), my brother, and I crammed into the back seat. Betty was thin, but still we literally rubbed elbows—and probably butts, too, though I've repressed that memory. Adding to this enforced awkward intimacy, Betty's long hair was usually wet in the mornings, so she flipped it constantly during the 30-minute trip to help it dry. I was immobilized, forced to smell wet hair, and, periodically, wet strands flicked me in the face.

A typical winter day was like this: John and I walked the mile to Mr. C's house in the freezing rain, arriving about 15 minutes early so that we'd never be the nuisance cause of any delay. We squeezed into the Bug, which was parked on the street, and waited there like out-of-favor stepchildren. John and I maybe vied with each other who could blow the longest plume of breath vapor until Mr. C emerged from the house and he and his children contorted themselves into the car. Then Mr. C would give the ignition a crank—and no go. Another try. Still no go. A third attempt. Again no.

. . . Houston, we have a problem. Please advise.

Bill, we're still running the numbers down here, but we advise that you try manual propulsion.

Manual propulsion? You mean "get out and push"?

That's affirmative.

So we're go for untethered EVA?

That's affirmative, Bill.

Copy that, Houston.

I should say at this point that the VW was parked on the street—headed downhill—for a reason. John and I and Mr. C's son would extricate ourselves, go behind the car, and give it as much thrust as we could. That was such an odd feeling—watching the vehicle we were supposed to be in coast away, leaving us farther and farther behind like ejected boosters. Usually, on Mr. C's third or fourth try, the clutch start technique would work and we'd hear the engine pop. We have ignition! Mr. C would orbit the block, pause, and we'd wrestle ourselves back in for the slow sputtering trek to school.

The afternoon return trips had an ambience all their own when as a special treat Mr. C would smoke a big cigar. Apollo 13 had more oxygen than we did. Houston, our capsule is filling up with smoke and noxious gases. Please advise.

German engineering, by way of rocket scientist Wernher Von Braun, got us to the moon, and, by way of automotive designer Ferdinand Porsche, got me to Mount de Sales.

Mr. C's VW Bug wasn't comfortable. It didn't run smoothly. And it certainly wasn't much to look at. But I guess I have to admit that it did move us through space when we needed it to—and in the end it brought us safely home.

How Hot I Am

During the 10 years or so that ratemyprofessors.com existed and that I was still teaching college English, not even one student reviewer ever awarded me a chili pepper icon indicating that she (or he) thought I was "hot."

In light of a recent *Maxim* magazine survey, I just don't understand this. *Maxim* asked a hundred women to complete the sentence "It's so hot when a man dot dot dots."

Two of the responders finished the sentence with "takes his shirt off." I'm thrilled by this answer and didn't know women were excited so easily. I take my shirt off at the end of every day. This means I also meet the hotness criterion of showing my "abs." Shouldn't that be ab? I don't know why this woman put an "s" on it. Who has more than one abdomen?

Another woman said, "It's so hot when a man wears the hell out of a T-shirt." You can ask my wife about this, but I once wore a T-shirt for over 20 years. At the end I'd had to cut the sleeves off, the cotton was gauzy thin, and the collar was separating. If that's not wearing the hell out of a T-shirt, I don't know what is. I also know "how to wear a suit." Duh.

Respondent #7, I do have a six-pack; it's in the refrigerator right now.

Respondent #45 finds it hot when a man "tells me what to do in the bedroom," and my wife can certainly vouch for this qualification. Why, just this morning in the bedroom I told her, "Baby, . . . make the bed."

To #18's answer "uses 'you're' and 'your' correctly on OK Cupid" I say, "You're in luck; I meet your standards."

I also mow the yard, act goofy, engage in witty banter, and have a weird talent.

It's true that many of the answers were predictable like "talks dirty," "spanks me during sex," "bites me," and "strips my panties with his mouth—slowly." Obviously, tremendous modesty prevents me from saying whether I do or do not meet THESE criteria.

But besides these predictable responses was this surprise: 5 of the hundred women surveyed chose as their answer "It's so hot when a man—cooks." Responder #3 added that when a man cooks for her, she wants "to bang him afterward." Ladies, I do cook. I love to grill sausage, ribs, ciabatta bread, and I cook a mean ribeye steak. Standing with my humongous spatula over blazing coals searing USDA Grade-A cow flesh, I honestly do not know how I could possibly be any hotter. I also microwave popcorn. I'm so glad to learn after all these years that the way to a woman's—"heart"—is through food preparation.

Gentlemen, if you can't stand being "hot," you better stay outta the kitchen.

And do I even need to say that 4 of the lusty *Maxim* women who took the survey indicated the way to *Maxim*-ize your hotness score—as you've probably guessed by now—is to be funny and make 'em laugh?

Am I Priority Male?

A year or two ago, the October/November issue of *AARP* magazine contained this helpful item—#45 in a list of "50 Ways to Stay Healthy" (p. 46): "Stamp out erection issues: Worry about impotency can cause . . . impotency. Here's a test to see if problems are physical or psychological. Wrap a length of postage stamps around the base of your penis. Secure the ends together and go to sleep. . . . If the stamps are torn along a perforation the next morning, you're still having good nocturnal erections."

I had high hopes when I gave this penis tip a try, but a few issues did come up.

1. The direction "Secure the ends together" is not specific enough. I don't want to get into details, but you should avoid staples and super glue.

2. When I woke, the 8 stamps (OK, 4) were still intact, but the words "Hazardous" and "Delivery Refused" had been stamped on my "package."

Also, the label "First Class" had been marked out and replaced with the handwritten designation "**Junk** Mail."

3. Because of the aforementioned super glue, the stamps are there to stay, so now I'm concerned my post might absolutely end up in Savannah overnight.

And what if postage *goes up*?
No worries. I bought Forever stamps.

Caller I.D. & Me

I rate Caller I.D. among the top 5 recent technology advancements that have made my life more livable. Since I know who's calling, I don't have to waste words, and I know what tone to answer in: "What the hell's the charge *this* time, officer?"

But even better than knowing *how* to answer, I know *whether* to answer. For example, I never answer when my voice caller I.D. warns me that "Breast Cancer" is calling. Why should I make it easy for Breast Cancer to reach me? I don't think so.

I'm also never going to pick up the phone when an entire city tries to contact me. Lately, Phoenix, Arizona has been the peskiest city wanting to talk to me, but I bet I've been called by over half the major cities in the United States.

Some of my favorite I.D.'s are the ones that indicate defrauders are trying to dupe me—I.D.'s such as "Invalid Number," "Not Assigned," or "Not in Service." Sometimes the identification is even more blatant. This might be hard to believe, but several times I've been dialed up by "Phone Scam." I LOVE Caller I.D.

I also like it when the scammers are more devious but not so clever that they don't give themselves away. Often my phone displays a local number with the same area code and first 3 digits as my own at the same time that my telephone's robotic secretary announces, "Out of Area." They want me to think they're in the neighborhood, but they're not being very neighborly. Though these calls annoy me, they also make me feel inflated pride in my amazing Sherlockian sleuthing skill.

Caller I.D. has also defended me against the most obnoxious of all my harassing callers, some guy identified by my phone only as "Spencer, Bill." As I said, since I got

Caller I.D., not even scam calls have bothered me much, but the fact that I call myself from my own number is just creepy. It's coming from *inside* the house. Somehow he has my number, but I've got *his* number, too, if you know what I mean. I've repeatedly not taken his calls, but he won't take the hint. Bill Spencer is pig-headed.

If he really wants to talk to me that much, shouldn't he do it face-to-face? Why not in person? Why on the phone? Is that sonuvabitch trying to *record* our conversations? It's my own number, so I can't even block the jerk.

On top of everything else, he keeps calling at the most inconvenient times, almost as if he knows exactly what I'm doing at any given moment. One thing he does that I especially hate is he'll call right after I hang up from talking to someone else. It's like he's saying, "I *know* you're there, Bill. Answer the damn phone!"

So, if you're reading this, Bill Spencer, I'm on to you. You're an inconsiderate creep, and as curious as I am to see what I have to say to myself, as much as I'm intrigued about what urgent message I seem so stubbornly intent on delivering to myself, I'm never going to answer. I don't care how good-looking, or brilliant, or hilariously funny you probably are; I'm not picking up the phone. Ever.

Brushes with the Law

I must just look guilty. Judging by my many encounters with the authorities you'd think I was some kinda outlaw. But I'm one of the most law-abiding, upstanding citizens I know. Not that that's any credit to me. If you know you're going to get caught—even when you're not doing anything—it's easy to walk the straight and narrow.

It started when I was in first grade. We went to the restroom 5 boys at a time with 4 of us waiting outside the door for our turn. Against the rules, one of us was talking—NOT me!—but we all got spanked by the substitute teacher. I've never forgotten the injustice of it.

When I was a teenager, three of my friends and I went to an outdoor Debbie Boone concert. Our folding chair seats were way in the back, and we saw that many people were standing up closer to the stage, so we moved to the front. One of my friends—I'll call him "the alleged suspect"—started yelling at Debbie to get her attention, something along the lines of "Hey, Debbie! Hey, Debbie! Hey, Debbie! You light up my life!" Soon, a police officer ambled over and asked me,"Are your tickets to the *next* show?" I said," No, officer, we have tickets to *this* show." Then he narrowed his eyes at me and said, "Well, keep it down." I've never forgotten the injustice of it.

I'm ashamed to confess that I have actually broken speed limit laws a few times in my life. Well, I'm not ashamed that I broke them; I'm ashamed at how the speeding tickets make me look like an over-cautious granny. Once I received a ticket for going a hellacious 32 miles per hour (*not* in a school zone, by the way). I distinctly remember that I had sped up because a school bus was impatiently tailgating me. Another time, I had been stopped at a red light for about a minute when blue lights started flashing behind me. (My wife will vouch for this.) I have to say, I was surprised. By the way, when a police officer asks if you know how fast you were going, "How *fast* I was going?! I was stopped!" is probably not the most prudent answer. My wife used to look over at the speedometer when I was driving and sigh in disgust at how slow I was, but she's given that up. She now accepts as fact that if I'm speeding, I *will* get pulled over. Every time I get behind the wheel, I feel the injustice of it.

My most recent brush with the law involves my exercise of my First Amendment right to peaceful protest. Several fellow troublemakers and I have been assembling every week at our town's main intersection to display our signs and wave to passers-by. After Charlottesville, our town passed an ordinance that signs couldn't be attached to anything that could possibly serve as a weapon. Because of the "Please arrest me; I must be guilty of something" aura that I give off, I knew I'd better toe the line. But I also wanted my sign to be readable from a distance. So I found a sturdy cardboard tube and attached my "Trump is a Porn-Again Christian" poster to that. This was a tube. Hollow. Made of paper. With no sharp edges. So I was surprised when the local police chief got out of her big black SUV with the dark-tinted windows and started walking toward me, looking straight at *me*. When she got within a few steps, she said, "Oh, I see what it is. Someone called to complain that you were out here with your sign on a stick." Then after looking more closely, she said, "But that cardboard *is* heavier than we'd like." I can see it now, having to answer a fellow con who's asking, "What are you in for?" I'll say, "Possession and brandishing of a cardboard tube with intent to provoke Trump supporters." I'm sure he'll say, "Whoa!" as he raises his hands and starts slowly backing away.

Determined not to give in on this issue, I hit upon a solution. If you drive by the old courthouse in my town during lunch hour on any Wednesday, you'll see me on the side of the road. I'll be the protestor holding a sign attached to a long, vibrant-blue, foam pool noodle. And, yes, my noodle is a bit floppy. Yes, it does waggle. And, yes, I am now known in certain circles as "the noodle guy." Go ahead and laugh. I do. And this time I feel like *I'm* having the *last* laugh.

And I love the justice of it.

Nobody Knows the Trebles I've Seen

f (forte)

I'm not one to toot my own horn, but when I started playing trumpet at the age of seventeen without any previous musical background whatsoever, many people told me they expected me to go far. "The farther the better," they said. "You should go on the road—right away," they said. More than one person suggested I take my trumpet playing overseas.

mf (mezzo-forte)

I started trumpeting as a senior in high school. We weren't good enough to play and march at the same time, so we were the Mount de Sales Stationary Band. Our first way-cool gig was at a PTA meeting, and I could hear two newly joined members *humming* the tune we were attempting through their clarinets.

Our second gig was playing for a significant community event—a house moving. The house was being moved from five blocks away to just across from our school. Yes, our high school band didn't move, but the house we played for did. We should have played "She's a Brick House" or "Our house is a very, very fine house," but we didn't. Instead, we played the only tune we knew at the time—"Aura Lee." Music to get jacked-up by.

mp (mezzo-piano)

To help me overcome my lack of musical experience and be less of a detriment to the band, I began taking trumpet lessons from a local "conservatory of music." This august institution doubled as the apartment of the owner/sole teacher. He had neighbors above and on each side, so most of my early instruction centered around playing as quietly as possible. I would miss notes and had a lousy tone, but my teacher would say, "That's good. Just try to play quieter. If you play softly, it'll be easy to get louder later." In retrospect, this reminds me of the line from the movie *Dodge Ball* "If you can dodge a hammer, you can dodge a ball."

p (piano)

I practiced faithfully, and an odd thing began happening to my lips. Playing a brass instrument actually builds up lip muscles, but because my embouchure wasn't right, the left side of my upper lip bulked up noticeably more than the right side. It looked as if Arnold Schwarzenegger was training the left side, while Richard Simmons had charge of the right.

My conservatory teacher invited me to join a small musical ensemble he'd put together, and our most memorable engagement was as the entertainment for a convention of chiropractors. Electronic keyboard, a guitar, a few winds and brasses, and for percussion—the periodic smack of cracking backs. We got off to a shaky start, stopped and, before continuing, had to make several "*adjustments.*"

pp (pianissimo)

People will tell you that playing a musical instrument is its own reward. They'll tell you this because you're not going to receive any other rewards, like fame or money or praise. I only ever received one compliment, and, ironically, I received it most often when I'd be feeling I wasn't sounding all that good. I can't tell you how important this reassurance was to keep me from giving up music altogether. I'd be discouraged, downhearted, and my band leader'd say, "Bill, you're sharp. You're really, really sharp."

ppp (pianississimo)
I say I played the trumpet, but "played" isn't really the right word. Performing on a musical instrument has very little to do with playing and everything to do with working. "Do you still work the trumpet?" people should ask me, and to compliment musicians they should say, "Rachelle, you work the piano so beautifully" or "Jack works the guitar like a house afire."

Decrescendo
Yes, I still play the trumpet. Sometimes. From a zen point of view. On the advice of teachers, bandmates, friends, my parents, my brothers, my wife, and a surprising number of complete strangers, I practiced playing more and more softly, more quietly and more quietly still until finally I accomplished the ambitious musical goal first set out for me, the perfection my audience kept urging me to and believed I could achieve—the harmonious perfection of absolute silence.

Please Give Me a Sign

"God/Universe, please make it clear to me whether I should take this position; please give me an unmistakeable sign," I thought as I headed to a job interview at what I will call Putrescence University (not its real name).

I had just retired from 25 years of teaching English at a university in Mississippi, but I was only 49 and not totally used up yet. Though I had sent out several applications, only Putrescence had called and scheduled an on-campus visit.

I met with the department Chair and liked him immediately, but his office was tiny, and the windowless, tiny next-door office—potentially mine—had no bookshelves. I didn't like the look of that. Was I right to be worried, or was I being too shelf-centered?

Remembering some recent friction back at my former university, I asked if the department was collegial: "Do the English professors get along?"

"Well," he responded, "I like myself." He then explained that at that moment *he* was the *only* active full-time English professor left amidst a spate of retirements and departures. "I don't like the sound of that," I thought to myself.

My wife joined us for a campus tour. First stop: the performing arts center. This PAC was the oddest one I've ever seen. It was wide enough, but there were only about a fourth of the rows of seats I expected. The auditorium looked comically truncated. Was it only for *short* performances? Our host explained that the building donor had gotten PO'd at PU during construction and had cut off funding.

Next stop: the library. When my wife and I entered, we noticed plenty of computer stations but very few books. We figured the book collection must be on a second floor and we simultaneously looked up to locate it—but there wasn't any upper floor. "Books and journals are very expensive," our host explained.

Our final stop was the administration building. This was a beautiful old building with a lot of architectural interest. Finally, a positive sign. The building was nice inside, too, but as we walked up the stairs to the second floor, my wife and I were stunned. At the top of the steps was a glassed-in room cram-packed with stuffed African big game animals. But what we noticed first—what nobody climbing the stairs could possibly escape noticing—was the taxidermied head and full neck of a full-grown giraffe mounted in the stairwell. My mouth fell open. "Who would shoot a giraffe and why?" I wondered. Our tour guide explained that one of the university's biggest benefactors made his support contingent on PU's keeping all of his still-growing collection of dead animals on prominent display.

It was a relief to exit Giraffic Park, and once outside, we noticed that several white canopies had been pitched nearby and that several workers were spreading dark mulch in the flower beds and alongside the sidewalks. "They're getting ready for our Founder's Day celebration tomorrow," our guide said, and then he took his leave but encouraged us to continue exploring on our own.

The white tents looked really festive, and I said to my wife, "This place has its problems, but the people are nice. Maybe a job here is better than no job at all?"

"Are you serious?" she said.

At this moment I became aware that the air was filled with something. I didn't like the smell of it.

"Do you smell that?" I asked my wife.

"Yeah, I smell it. How could I not?"

"What is it?"

"I'm not sure. It smells like . . . It smells like manure."

She was right. It did smell like manure. And now we realized that the "mulch" that was being spread all over campus was in fact cow manure. Pretty *fresh* cow manure. Workers were preparing to celebrate the founding of this university by making the entire campus literally stink.

We soon wandered behind the administration building, where we saw it: the mother lode—a fifteen-foot-high pyramidal pile of manure. After a few seconds my wife said, "There's some symbolism for you, Mr. Literature Teacher. This job is one big pile of bullshit."

The Universe had given me my sign.

And it had a sense of humor.

An Alarming Trend

I don't own a cell phone. Seriously. No GPS either. No apps. I don't own an iAnything. The speed of technological change intimidates me, and the prospect of becoming an addicted screen zombie scares the bejeezus out of me. I thought I should confess all this so you'd know exactly what you're dealing with.

Some years ago my wife, stepson, and I visited my wife's twin sister (Sissy) and her retired neurosurgeon husband in their beautiful new home in Alabama. Sissy, as a birthday gift for my stepson, had arranged for him (and me) to go on a 4-hour guided fishing tour on a local lake. As we were leaving, Sissy gave me the key to the house and said she and my wife were going shopping. When I asked about the house security system, Sissy said they'd be back before our return, but she assured me she wouldn't activate the alarm anyway so there was nothing to worry about. Then she asked, "You have the code, don't you?"

"I do have the code—somewhere—in my wallet," I admitted.

"Never mind. You won't need it. I'm not going to set the alarm," she said again.

Our fishing guide said the lake was full of bass and bream, but what we caught was bupkis. It was so hot and the fish were so uncooperative that my stepson insisted on ending the outing two hours early.

When we got back to the house, we saw from the missing car that the twins were still out. I unlocked the door, entered, and then noticed that the alarm control box had begun flashing red. "Oh, God, the alarm is armed!" I knew I had 30 seconds to deactivate it, and as the rate of red flashing increased, I rifled in a panic through my wallet for the scrap of paper with the code on it.

Whatever complaints I might have about Sissy's house alarm, I have to admit that its sound system was state-of-the-art. The entire neighborhood could clearly hear the robotic-voiced message that followed: "INTRUDER ALERT. THE POLICE HAVE BEEN CALLED. LEAVE THE AREA IMMEDIATELY!" I myself think 5 or even 3 repetitions would be enough to scare off burglars, but this warning blared over and over for the next 15 minutes. The decibel level was so high and the repetition so relentless that even if the police had *not* been called, crooks would still have scrammed just to escape the painful, maddening racket.

Despite the persistent advice to "leave the area immediately," I decided to stay and face the law. I didn't want the police to have to come looking for me so I went out to the end of the driveway, and I begged my stepson to stick close to me since I thought I looked much less suspicious with a kid by my side. I'm pretty sure I put my arm around him.

A police officer did soon arrive, and he ominously parked so as to block my exit. They may call it a security system, but somehow I wasn't feeling all that secure. I quickly began explaining the situation: have key, didn't expect alarm to be set, visiting wife's twin sister and her retired neurosurgeon husband. . . . The officer interrupted me at this point and said, "He's retired and you're married to twins? You don't look old enough to be retired."

It's funny how the mind works.

My mind went into a kind of paradoxical racing slow motion. "Why did I mention the retirement detail? That's not even relevant. This policeman is a highly trained lie detector, and he right now thinks he's caught me in a lie. He might be taking me downtown if I don't start doing some serious tap dancing." I remember thinking of what I had to do in those terms—tap dancing. I was on a stage. I had a suspicious audience. "Feet don't fail me now!" In one breath without any pauses I said, "He retired early for medical reasons, and he's several years older than his wife, and I'm younger than mine." All this was true, and despite my nervousness, my interrogator bought it and drove off.

"Whew! Thank God that's over!" I thought as my stepson and I walked back to the house. That infernal alarm had finally stopped, and I said out loud, "That was a close one" as we for a second time entered the house.

The tech savvy among you probably know what happened next, but me, I didn't see it coming. As I realized a few seconds later, the alarm system included inside-the-house motion detectors. How did I realize this? It was because of a subtle hint, really: fifteen more delightful minutes of "INTRUDER ALERT. THE POLICE HAVE BEEN CALLED. LEAVE THE AREA IMMEDIATELY!"

Those were the actual words, but what I heard was something of a translation—a loud, repeated, insistent message from the Universe: "Bill Spencer, you should be alarmed—because when it comes to technology, you, sir, are an idiot.

Group Foot Massage

Just so you know, I've never been into outrageously kinky public anything with anybody. But when several women at the writers' conference I was attending began soliciting participation in a session of group foot massage, my interest was piqued.

There wasn't a lot of information—just a time and a room number—so my imagination filled in the details. The way I pictured it was that I would lie barefoot on a bed while the women took turns lovingly kneading and caressing my feet, probably with warmed, scented massage oils and lotions— perhaps even drying my feet with their long, silky hair. I would luxuriate in the attention and become so relaxed that I would nearly drift off to sleep while still reveling in the sensuality of the experience. And it also occurred to me— being at a writers' conference and all—that as a bonus I was definitely going to get something to write about out of this. So I agreed to join in. And so did my wife.

Should I bathe before going or at least wash my feet? Should I give myself a pedicure? Should I take my own lotion? Should I wear special socks and shoes? Would sandals be too much of a tease? Or should I just pad down the hallway boldly barefoot and arrive ready to go?

When my wife and I arrived, there were three or four women and two men already in the room. I can't tell you how disappointed I was to see the other men. They didn't fit in with my imagined scenario at all.

There were two beds, and lying on one of them was a large, colorful foot reflexology chart with lines marking off body systems that different areas of the feet corresponded to. The areas had such designations as "lungs," "stomach," "bladder," coccyx," ascending colon," "sigmoid colon," and "descending colon."

The romance of my vision was starting to slip away.

One of the other men, however—whose expectations may have been similar to my own—had brought champagne and proposed we share some before getting started. The bottle was not chilled, but he said, "That's not a problem because I brought ice to put in our cups." He popped the cork, and what followed is one of the strangest things I've ever seen. A stream of froth and foam shot out with such violence that the bottle leaped out of the uncorker's hands, flipped upside down, and did a hypnotic cobra dance up and down in midair for about five seconds before crashing to the floor.

With the formal toasting out of the way, we got down to the ceremony itself.

One of the women called our attention to the reflexology chart, explained that whatever bodily problems we had could be helped by massaging the appropriate foot-bottom area, and then encouraged us to get right to work. The women removed their shoes, sat on the beds and began rubbing their own feet. Yes, their *own* feet! Maybe I should've pressed for more details before giving my consent. This was obscene.

From the women's conversation, I gathered that they especially had issues with indigestion. "How can things get any worse than this?" I wondered. Then I noticed the women were rubbing the "stomach" areas on their feet. After a few moments, I heard a burp. Then another. Soon there was a cacophony of belching. The room sounded like a frog pond.

Now although I had felt close enough to these women to let them caress my feet, this was *too* intimate. What was my safe word?

Call me old-fashioned, but I think you should be married to someone before you engage in unrestrained burping with them, and even then it should be in private, just the two of you.

As small bursts of belly gas exploded all around me, the last vestige of my fantasy disintegrated. Disillusioned, and in despair over the nature of the universe, I stared for a moment at my toes. Then I took a deep breath and fell to work, rubbing the ball of my left foot—right in the "heart" area.

After all—my naive heart was broken.

Bill Spencer

Habitat for (Oh, the) Humanity!

In my idealistic, full-of-youthful-promise twenties, I decided to make the world a better place—by volunteering with Habitat for Humanity. I was determined to help create homes for deserving families. I just needed to learn in exactly what capacity I could best advance humankind. My paid job at the time was teaching English, so all I had to do was figure out how my enviable skill at reading literature and grading compositions was transferable. Constructing a house, constructing an essay—there *had* to be significant parallels.

When I first showed up to my volunteer job, I was assigned to actual construction work. Since in my teens I had built a two-dog doghouse, I felt pretty confident I could manage driving nails into boards—as long as someone coached me on how many nails and exactly where. The problem was that the supervisor I required obviously could have accomplished more with less frustration had I not been "helping."

After I'd been hammering for a while, a couple of veteran workers showed up, and that's when I learned how dangerous a thing it is to volunteer. One had a pistol with a rubber plunger-like contraption at the end of the barrel for shooting bolts into concrete. The other worker had a pneumatic nail gun. There were guns to the left of me and guns to the right. Once, when Mr. Nail Gunner got too close to the edge of a board, a nail zipped past me only a few feet from my head. A few feet's difference and I'm pretty sure an x-ray of my skull with a nail sticking in it would have ended up on the internet. If you've guessed I asked to be reassigned after this close brush with cranial skewering, then you've hit the nail right on the head.

So I was moved to demolition. An old house had been donated to Habitat, and it needed to be renovated and moved. I was assigned to tear out a wall with a crow bar. This sounded like a lot of fun. Who doesn't relish the idea of destroying another person's hard work? But this was an *old* house. The walls were not just sheet rock and insulation. They were made of heavy bat board, and I could not pry these boards loose. All I could do was break them into smaller and smaller jagged pieces. After an entire morning's work, I had made so little progress that the job boss decided to keep the wall after all.

After this house was moved, I was sure I'd finally found my proper niche when I was tasked with cleaning up debris at the original site. I raked and gathered small chunks of concrete and splinters of wood. "This is well within my skill set," I thought, "and no one's shooting at me, so it's absolutely safe." That's what I thought—until another volunteer, who'd brought his front-end loader, scooped and then lifted the left-behind multi-ton concrete front steps. He lifted them high over his tractor's cab and then inched toward a waiting dump truck. The machine strained with the weight, and balance seemed to be an important issue as the driver maneuvered over to the truck. Once there, he had only to tip the steps forward, but whatever he was *trying* to do, what actually *happened* was that the massive concrete Sword of Damocles poised over his head began to rock—first rocking back toward him. I saw what was happening with that intense clarity of slow motion. The physicists among you may know the rate at which free-falling objects fall. I don't. But I knew that if the concrete steps rocked out of the scoop, they'd be *this* close to becoming a stairway to heaven.

Luckily, the rocking stopped, and finally the concrete death-threat thundered into the dump truck as planned. But I realized that even while voluntarily doing a good deed on your day off, you can be flat killed.

After this, I decided I was probably a painter. With painting, there'd be no guns, no projectiles, no harrowing life-or-death drama. I'd wear goggles and not sniff the paint too much, and I'd be fine. So on a Saturday morning I joined several women painting a bedroom. The soon-to-be homeowner had picked out the paint, so who was I to question the color? Is there even a term for maroon-tinged purple? The artists among you may know. I don't. But what I do know is that when the homeowner saw our full-day's work, she said, "Oh, God! That's not the color I picked. Can we change it?"

There are many competent, handy, fearless altruists who know how to further the admirable mission of Habitat for Humanity. But as you've probably deduced by now, *I* don't.

Yes, it feels good to make the world a better place. And that's exactly what I finally figured out how to do—the day I quit volunteering.

Maybe I'll try my hand as a humorist.

My Body & Organized Labor

My body has unionized. Every year I'm presented with more and more demands.

When I was young, I was able to exploit and abuse my body—make it work overtime without compensation. And I could make it do just about anything for minimum wage. But no more.

My stomach was the first to go Union. In the early stages of our contract negotiations, I thought I made it a fair offer, but it wouldn't even come to the table. Each time I pushed, it pushed back. Our dealings were so stressful I developed chronic heartburn. Finally, I had to swallow my pride. No more dairy. Ever. Not even a little bit. Then no onions. Then not too much fatty meat. My stomach union got bolder, and our contract list of required working conditions got so long it took me days to digest it: no garlic, no barbecue sauce, nothing with vinegar in it, including mustard and ketchup, not too much salt, no beans, no cabbage, no pickles, no chili—ever again, and alcoholic beverages only in the smallest doses and only for medicinal purposes. I'm not proud of my bargaining skills, but do you think you could've done any better? I mean these guys when *they* don't get their way, they throw acid at you.

Besides all the restrictions—my stomach started demanding more and more time off. Before the union, it had routinely put in 20-hour days. Did I want an extra dessert at 1 or 2 a.m.? "Piece o' cake," my stomach used to say. But that was when my stomach was still a teenager—before it had a family and lots of bills to pay. Our new contract calls for 7-hour shifts only: noon to 7 p.m. My stomach also now refuses to process big orders. And it wants benefits like a drug program providing antacids and Proton Pump Inhibitors. I'm at the union's mercy. What am I gonna do? Get another stomach? I'm over a barrel. What really hurts is that despite the many, many concessions I've made, there are some indications my stomach's still not happy. I've heard rumblings.

A couple of years ago my feet held their own big meeting, and the upshot was that I had to sweeten their deal. I've had to pad them with orthotic shoe inserts ever since. "A little cushion in the contract is just standard, Buddy," they told me. I realized that when it came to my feet's demands, I didn't have a leg to stand on. These are some rough, callous characters. I have to hand it to 'em: my feet've got balls.

Of all my body unions, the neck is the most unreasonable. For one thing, it wants to go out all the time. Our dealings require constant adjustments. I've had to agree not only to frequent rest breaks on pillows made to exact specifications, but—and I blush to say this—my cervical employee has demanded that it get *massages* all the time. Who *gets* perks like that? I held out as long as I could, but finally gave in. I'm so embarrassed I can hardly hold my head up.

There are of course other body parts that I've had to cajole and pressure to keep working for me, and I'd like to tell you about the delicate,very sensitive, very private negotiations we've had over the years. Unfortunately, I had to sign a nondisclosure agreement. All I can say is I never thought I'd live to see the day that a contract with a body part would include details about "mood," "variety," and "ambience."

Well that's about it—the story of my body's dealings, over 6 decades, with a powerful anatomical labor movement. I wanted to provide you with a clever, satisfying ending, but, I'm sorry to say, my brain just went on strike.

Life in the Woods

Partly influenced, I'm guessing, by Thoreau's *Walden*—twelve years ago my bride and I moved to the mountain woods of North Carolina. We, too, "wished to live deliberately." In my own experiment I've discovered that "life in the woods" is indeed mostly idyllic, but have also come to realize that ole Henry David might have glossed over a few unpleasant drawbacks to "a primitive and frontier life."

I could, for example, mention the multiflora, climbing wild roses with long flexible canes that take over everywhere. Multiflora, I learned, is known as an aggressive plant not only because of its invasive spreading habit. Once as I hacked through a thicket of these arching canes, a thorn hooked into my upper lip. Thoreau does describe fishing, but in *his* narrative he is the fish**er**, not the fish**ee**.

The Walden woods hermit also fails to "front" what for me has been *the* "essential fact of life" in the woods, namely insects. Sure, he describes a battle of some ants—but they're battling each other; he's not battling them. I've been bitten by mosquitoes, gnats, flies, and ants and have been stung by wasps, hornets, and yellow jackets, and right now, carpenter bees are enlarging the honeycomb of tunnels they have already chewed into the wood of my house.

The worst woodland insects don't just bite and run but instead come to stay for a visit: insects like chiggers—even the name is disturbing—which you can't see but which raise large itchy welts where they've burrowed under your skin. But at least chiggers voluntarily vacate the premises after a few days and at least you can't see their horrifying appearance. Neither of these ameliorations is true, however, of my least favorite essential fact of woodsy life,

. . . which is ticks. Ticks look like tiny bloody crabs. They crawl on you, stick their heads into your body, suck your blood, and afflict you with terrible diseases. I spread insect poison all around my cabin every spring, and still there they are. The woods are a ticking time bomb: tick, tick, tick.

You might think you could avoid the little suckers by staying out of high weeds, but several times I've found them crawling on the floors and walls of our kitchen. Once I even found one on my car's steering wheel. How does a tick get on the steering wheel of your car, and what's it doing there? Trying to *drive*!? Trying to drive me crazy!

Of course the most repulsive place to find ticks is on your own body. I was first introduced to these unwanted guests as I sat on our deck. Ticks dropped from tree branches above, landing on my head, neck, and shoulders like Black Ops forces. Paratrooper ticks! Thoreau didn't even hint at such a nightmare. We now refer to our deck as "tick town."

Once they've landed on you, they usually hightail it for your head since they like to hide in your hair, and once they get there, they "attach." I have found ticks crawling on nearly every part of my body. And just last summer—this is really true—I touched my nose and felt a scab where there was no scab, so I pinched and, sure enough, I had a hitchhiker.

Now as I said before, ticks are disseminators of disease, but the internet has reassured me that ticks need to be attached for more than 24 hours to infect their hosts. So your best defense against tick-borne disease is early detection—which further means your best defense is self-touching. A *lot* of self-touching. When you see a mountain man running his fingers through his hair, don't assume he thinks he's James Dean; he's probably just probing for parasites. When I pinched the tick off my nose, I pondered exactly where he was going. As I said before, ticks prefer hairy hideaways, so it occurred to me that his destination might have been my nose's *interior*. Now I'm not necessarily recommending routinely conducting tick touch tests inside your nostrils, but if you're in the woods, how could you risk *not* doing so? You just have to feel around; you don't have to pick.

At the end of *Walden*, Thoreau says he left the woods after two years for as good a reason as he went there. I'm betting . . . it was ticks.

Holding on to Old Ratty Things

Apparently, I've grappled with the problem of mortality from the age of four. My parents told me that I asked—probably triggered by an explanation about the death of my grandfather—"Why is God always making *new* people? Why doesn't he just keep the ones he's got?"

Just keeping what you've got has always made sense to me. In infancy I had a baby-blue security blanket—which I called my donny—that I dragged everywhere with me for years. I would have kept it longer, but when it deteriorated to what my father considered a disgustingly dirty piece of rag, he tossed it on a pile of burning pine straw. In a minute my donny was gone. I haven't felt secure since.

I drive a 23-year-old car, a 1997 Firebird with 190,000 miles on it. The dash is cracked, the upholstery faded. It has some leaks, too many dents and scratches to count, and sometime's there's a smell like burning oil—but I'm in no hurry to let it go. Firebirds aren't made anymore, and I truly cannot find a new car I like better.

Every Christmas, I decorate a tabletop Christmas tree that I bought for a dollar at W.T. Grant's 46 years ago. It sheds dozens of its glued-on green cellophane needles every year, getting thinner and thinner. But it looks absolutely fine—good even—after it's all decorated with a 20-year-old string of lights and with ornaments I've cherished for decades.

I owned a heavy-as-a-boulder cathode-ray-tube TV till just two years ago. While I was in bed with a stomach virus, my wife and stepson bought a flatscreen without telling me because they knew I'd think it wasteful—a shame even—to replace something that was working perfectly fine.

I realize these facts might make me sound like a hoarder or at the very least a quirky, must-have-lived-through-the-

Depression-era old coot. But in my view there's a lot at stake here. By holding on to old ratty things I'm trying to send a signal to my wife: "Baby, even though I have a long list of signs of wear, and could easily be replaced with a newer model—why not just hold on to me a little while longer?"

And of course I hope *God* is paying attention to my example as well. Why be in a hurry to replace people just because we've aged? Just because our needles have thinned? Just because we're bulky and overweight? Just because we have a few leaks and dents and could smell better?

A few Christmases ago, my wife gave me a new belt to replace the one I'd been wearing for twenty-five years. She had cleverly commissioned it to be made by a Hollywood movie prop company to look almost exactly like my old one, except that it wasn't about to break in half. The leather had been artificially aged; it was faded in color and *looked* old. I taught literature too many years for the symbolism to be lost on me. It made me feel . . . What's the word? Oh yeah—*distressed*.

OK, I'll admit it: I do wear the new belt.

As for the old belt? I haven't thrown it away. It's way, way back in a closet. Where I hope not even God can find it.

The Little Guy: An Unconscious Love Story

I've lived long enough now to confirm Jung's and Freud's theory of the existence of the *un*conscious, and I believe I've figured out how to better understand it. What I've realized is that it helps to think of the unconscious as "the little guy," while the conscious self is "the big guy." The little guy is like a hard-drinking independent contractor who lives in the ten-story library warehouse basement of our brains. He takes on lots of jobs but does them on his own schedule. To find the files on *people's names* and *movies you've seen that actor in before*, he has to climb a ladder that's on rollers, and he's not a fast climber. The *big* guy is like a CEO. He's in charge. He often asks the little guy to do jobs but knows he's not always dependable. He regards the little guy as a kind of idiot savant.

I was first clued in to this dynamic once when I woke up in the middle of the night to do what is referred to in genteel circles as "pay a visit to Uncle Blad," an uncle without peer, a regular wiz. I say "woke up," but actually only my *little* guy was awake. He's not very quick, what from being stuck in a basement and the heavy drinking, so he functions like an auto pilot. My bathroom was down the hall, and on this night the bedroom door was closed and my wife had hung clothes on the back of the door that covered the doorknob. So my little guy, who had steered me to the bathroom countless times with no trouble, this time *had* trouble. He groped for the doorknob, but could not find it. I imagine my little guy talked to himself: "Uh oh. The door's closed. Door knob? Door knob? Where's the door knob? Hmmm. Looks like I'm gonna have to wake up the big guy." Which he did, and the big guy took over.

I bet you, too, have experienced this dynamic when driving. Many's the time my conscious self has delegated the driving to my unconscious. The little guy's poor about keeping a steady speed and he's zoomed right past intended exits, but he's pretty good at keeping the car between the painted lines and avoiding wrecks. This arrangement has allowed my big guy to indulge in more interesting mental pursuits, like figuring out ways to help my mother, before she died, be happier; and imagining new humor column topics.

Whatever deficiencies my little guy might have, I forgive him—because in certain areas, such as feelings, he's a savant rather than an idiot. I realized this truth some months after I began spending a lot of time with Carolyn. We weren't exactly dating. We were in graduate school together in Knoxville, and she had no car. So I was taking her and her son to Shoney's for supper and then to Kroger for groceries. The three of us also went to the circus and the zoo that fall. We looked like a family and were often mistaken for one. But I knew Carolyn had at least two other suitors besides an estranged husband back in Minnesota.

Then came a winter day—the second day in a row that university classes were canceled for snow. On the first snow day, Carolyn, her four-year-old son wearing my cowboy hat (which fit him), and I—had had a great time playing in the snow. A great time. But we made no plans for the next day. On that second snow day, as I walked into a Walgreen's near campus, I saw Carolyn with another man who I knew was after her. Now before this moment, the fact that other men were pursuing her hadn't consciously bothered me even though I admired and liked Carolyn very much. But at this moment my unconscious shot a message up to my conscious self, a message that went like this: "You idiot. You dumb, stupid idiot. Why didn't you ask Carolyn to spend today w' *you*? I got news for you, Buddy. You're in love with her. You *been* in love with her, you nincompoop."

Now I'm as surprised as you are at the little guy's harsh language and derogatory tone that day—but I have to admit he was within his rights. Who was he, he thought, to tell his *boss* he was in love? Wasn't that something so important that a CEO should know without a basement employee, a lowly functionary, having to tell him? My little guy must have watched in frustration and disgust for days, weeks even, before his outburst. Who can blame him? I don't.

Have I rambled on too long? I'm sorry. I wasn't conscious of it.

Indoor Skydiving on My Honeymoon

I went indoor skydiving on my honeymoon. I mean that literally, not figuratively.

But let me back up and say first that I'm afraid of heights—at least I'm afraid whenever I think there's some danger of dying as a result of those heights.

So of course one of my early dates with my future bride was mountain climbing. After two hours of hiking up the steep Chimney Tops trail in the Smoky Mountains, Carolyn and I arrived at the final challenge—a nearly vertical rock face. I didn't like the look of it. Signs warned that some people had fallen to their deaths, so I confessed my phobia and revealed my wimpiness to the woman I most wanted to admire me. She was disappointed. I sat at the bottom of the rock face while Carolyn scampered up it like a mountain goat. A very attractive mountain goat, mind you. One with whom I'd be happy to have kids.

For our honeymoon a couple of years later, we were back in the Smokies—Gatlinburg—and Carolyn's desire to try indoor skydiving would be my chance to redeem myself, my chance to demonstrate to my bride that her husband was a man who could master his fears and be a man. I was married to an adventurer now, so I, too, would be an adventurer—unafraid, confident, someone who shared her interests and matched her spirit. Yes, this is the interior pep talk that cycled in my mind as we drove to Flyaway Indoor Skydiving in Pigeon Forge, which turned out to be an odd cylindrical building about four stories high.

The first step in my quest to become an intrepid indoor sky flyer involved a 20-minute "training" video that was apparently produced by a high-powered team of lawyers. There were in fact some training tips, but the main gist of the video was to ensure that by the end of it, even if I were an awfully slow learner, it could easily be proven in a court of law that I fully understood all of the dangers my honeymoon adventure might entail. The oft-repeated refrain of the video was "You could be injured—OR EVEN DIE." That's the way the video narrator said it, with a dramatic pause and a deepening and intensifying of his voice when he got to the "OR EVEN DIE" part. The third time I heard this, my confidence began to waver. By the fifth time, my fears were resurfacing, and by the tenth time, I was convinced, "This is it. I'm gonna die."

At the end of the video we were led into a small room, where in turn we were told to sit in a chair in front of a video camera so that there'd be a video record of our signing the legal release form that said, "Neither I nor my heirs will sue Flyaway Indoor Skydiving regardless of what happens to me—even if I am injured—OR EVEN DIE." The new wrinkle that caught my attention here was the reference to "heirs." Heirs? I didn't have any heirs. Didn't one have to be dead to have . . . ? Oh.

In phase two, we moved into the equipment room, where it was explained that we'd be flying in a vertical wind tunnel with a metal mesh floor, beneath which was a giant fan that could produce wind speeds up to 200 mph. We were warned to empty our pockets and to remove all jewelry since anything that fell off of us and hit the fan blades would be shot back up in our direction as a bullet-like projectile. This sounded like Russian roulette to me. What if a filling fell out while I was screaming?

We donned blousy nylon jumpsuits, goggles, and foam earplugs and were ready to begin our three-minute turns in the wind tunnel along with two men on the Flyaway staff. Were they spotters? Or had long practice determined that it took two men to drag away the lifeless bodies?

Too soon my turn came to step into the roaring tower. My bride watched through the small window of thick glass.

It comforted me to know that she would witness my demise, could attest to my courage until the very end.

I stood in the center, the sweet spot, huge blades whirring below me. The fan revved, and the wind roared louder. The staffers cupped my elbows. The fan cranked higher. Still higher. Then I leapt up. Leapt into the prescribed posture of an arched spread eagle, a diver of the sky, a soaring paratrooper. And I lifted off. Saw she was smiling, she my wife now for twenty-nine years. I rose. I was flying. Flying.

And I haven't landed yet.

Relativity

My Wife Is an Alien

My wife, Carolyn, is the best wife in the universe. I say "in the universe" deliberately because, you see, Carolyn is not originally from this planet. Now I can't vouch for the truth of the claim that women are from Venus and Bruno is from Mars, but I do believe I've amassed enough evidence to convince you regarding my spouse from space.

First, you should know that Carolyn is a twin, an identical twin. Yes, identical. A clone maybe? Or perhaps on her home planet, babies always come in identical pairs.

The twin thing is provocative enough, but I didn't really begin to see the light until Carolyn let slip a few telling remarks. One day (and often since then) she announced, "I love living on a planet with wind." It's true that this could partly be explained as an exercise in New Agey gratitude—but why not just say, "I love wind" or "I love *the* wind"?

Her sleeping habits are even more suspicious. Carolyn untucks the sheets so that she can stick her feet out free of any covers. She says she can't sleep if her feet are hot. (My feet, *on the other hand*, must be warm.) When she noticed the socks on my feet and the multiple blankets, she actually asked me—I'm not kidding about this—"How can you breathe?" Now, I understand that mouth-breathers are fairly common on this planet, but surely foot-breathers have to be extraterrestrials.

As far as eating, my cosmic companion *usually* remembers to conform to local customs, but there was one time that she, her twin, and I stopped at a McDonald's for cheeseburgers. After we took our order to a table, I went back for ketchup. Roughly twenty seconds later, as I walked back toward the table, I was met halfway by the twins who somehow had fully consumed the cheeseburgers and were ready to leave. I can only guess at how they absorbed the caloric McFuel, but I'm quite sure no mastication was involved. I had to eat *my* burger the old-fashioned way—in the car.

My wife also has an inhuman sense of smell (as does her twin, of course). Once she told me she smelled a dead fish in the attic. I was delighted at the chance finally to prove her wrong, so I did a thorough search, of course found no fish, and gloated over her mistake—until two days later when I noticed a fish carcass on the roof of our house, apparently carried there from our recently flooded ditch by some bird of prey. Another time, in the car, her sister said, "I smell a grass fire," and my wife said, "Yes, but with a little burning garbage mixed in." About two miles down the road, we came to a large grass fire, in the midst of which a single barrel of garbage was also ablaze. My wife's sense of smell is so unearthily keen that she has repeatedly insisted, "I can smell myself from far away."

But what most convinces me about my wife's off-planet origins is her psychic ability. She keeps track of noises and time *in her sleep.* She sometimes has the same dreams as her twin. She knows when our neighbor is about to call. She correctly "foretold" at a Halloween fortune-telling that one of our students was pregnant though the student vehemently denied it. She sees "ghosts." And, most disturbingly, she sometimes answers questions that I'm thinking but have not verbalized. So she clearly can read my mind, which is an awfully creepy place to have access to.

I firmly believe in the claim that somewhere there's a perfect somebody for everybody. In my case, the Supplier of Perfect Somebodies had to range a little farther afield than usual. Yes, my wife is light years beyond any earthling woman. She is truly stellar. Actually, make that "*inter*stellar."

My Bewitching Wife

I can't say for certain whether my wife is a witch or not, but I do know she charmed me when I first saw her and she does have a "weird sister." (Sorry, Sissy. That's just a little witches-in-*Macbeth* humor.) I also know that at least a few of Carolyn's students wondered about her.

You see, Carolyn stood out as quite different in the Mississippi Delta, where we were both teaching college English. One of her son's teachers—upon seeing Carolyn dressed in a black broom skirt, black turtleneck, long black coat, black scarf, black boots, and a black fedora—actually said, "You're not from around here, are you?" Most of Carolyn's wardrobe is indeed black. She looks great in this color, and she says her style is a holdover from her poorer days when she discovered it as a way to disguise how few clothes she owned. She taught in black clothing so much that even her freshmen noticed it.

So one day in English 102, a research-essay class in which Carolyn's students were required to investigate some paranormal topic—say the Salem Witch Trials, for example—one student started joking around with her. This is when another student joined in the banter and cautioned his classmate not to "mess with" the teacher: "Haven't you noticed she always wears black? You better watch your step, man. No tellin' *what* she might do." Although all of this was said in fun, the warned student did quiet down and become more subdued and started looking at Carolyn a little differently.

The very next morning as Carolyn was driving through campus, she noticed that one of the hundreds of tree frogs that plagued us had somehow gotten inside her car and was making itself an intolerable nuisance by hopping around like crazy. Quick-handed from swatting so many Delta mosquitoes, Carolyn was able to grab the frog, roll down her window, and fling it outside almost all in one motion. When she glanced to see its trajectory, she was dismayed to see it land squarely on a male student passing on the sidewalk. *Then* she noticed that the male student was the same one who had been warned the day before of Carolyn's alleged preternatural powers. The look on his face was one of astonishment. He may have been wondering if the frog (or was it a newt?) clinging to his chest was an ordinary frog or was it a previously troublesome student now transmogrified. Carolyn, realizing how so many unlikely coincidences all converged in this moment, could not help laughing (what may have even sounded like cackling) as she rode away.

As I said at the outset, I don't really know if my wife is a witch. All I know for certain is that she has continued to enchant me for over 29 years and that I'm still—happily—under her spell.

Shortcut to Urubamba

Would you like to think globally but stay locally? Then you should follow in my footsteps. I got the benefits of trotting the globe without the risks and hassles. Instead of *being* a world traveler, I just married one.

Yes, my wife is a cosmopolite, who has suffered the giardia, chronic salmonella, and blood amoebas to prove it. I guess that's why they call it the travel "bug." I know what you're thinking: "Sure, she has some digestive issues, but was she ever detained in Peru as a suspected terrorist because the border police had a picture of a terrorist who looked just like her?" I'm surprised you'd even ask since the answer is so obviously "Of course she was." And don't bother asking if she lived among tarantulas and scorpions, or swam with piranha and caimans, or killed a bushmaster with her flipflop. You already know the answer. (By the way, "bushmaster" is a deadly pit viper, not a weed eater or some studly actor's porn name.) The point is you don't have to travel thousands of miles and spend thousands of dollars to sprinkle your conversation with words like "caimans."

I've learned a lot about foreign culture and customs from Carolyn's Peace Corps stories of Brazil—from the comfort of my own home. I'm fascinated by the varying attitudes about what you can and can't touch in different corners of the world. She explained that Brazilians have different ideas about personal space. When she was standing on a crowded bus, locals routinely would feel her hair, which looked straighter and perhaps softer than their own. Touching a stranger's body in public wasn't just acceptable in Brazil; it was customary. As people engaged in tête-à-têtes with her, they'd pat her tummy with the back of their hands. This just meant "I'm talking to you."

While one's tummy was up for grabs, one's house decidedly was not. Knocking on the door of a Brazilian's house is taboo. The custom there is to stand several feet away from the door and to clap your hands to let the residents know you've arrived for a visit. This might sound strange, but until you've tried it, don't knock it.

Carolyn told me she met a Peace Corps volunteer stationed in Africa who said house-touching was also verboten where she served. Instead, she had to stand outside the home and loudly yell, "Conk, conk! Conk, conk!" These various door-knocking customs strike me as the basis for a hit kindergarten song, one with a "Knock, knock, clap, clap, conk, conk" refrain.

Ignorance of foreign customs can get actual travelers into trouble. One of Carolyn's Peace Corps compatriots once killed time waiting on a city street corner by snapping his finger and then slapping his right fist into his left palm. He was soon arrested for obscene gesturing in public. Apparently, what he was doing was the equivalent of brazenly flipping off every passer-by. It was if he was muttering, "Screw you, screw you, and screw you, too!"

Sure, it's cool to be able to say, "When I was in Urubamba . . . ," but it's also cool to say, "When my *wife* was in Urubamba . . . ". And you can say the latter without subjecting yourself to possible incarceration, eye-water-drinking bugs, or the risk of malaria.

So let your travel-hungry spouses be your passport to a cosmopolitan education. Encourage them to go on trips to Dubrovnik, the Cinque Terre, and the Ring of Kerry with like-minded others. As for *you*, sail down the Amazon on your La-Z-Boy. Take the Grand Tour from your futon. Get on board the S.S. Sofa for your secret shortcut to safe adventure.

Your journey begins with a single step—a single step down the aisle.

Never Spank Your Skunk

When your twin sister calls you to help get rid of a gang of 9-12 smell-raising skunks living under her porch, you go—so my wife went out to Nogal, New Mexico. I call them a "gang," but the technical term for a skunk group is "surfeit." Some comedian probably came up with that term since almost everyone considers even one skunk a surfeit.

My wife's sister, whom we call "Sissy," was trying to sell her very pricey ranch house but knew that the sulfurous stench of about a dozen skunks might possibly discourage would-be buyers.

Step one in the elimination of these vile-smelling varmints—the research phase—turned up the internet advice "Never spank your skunk" since it's a spiteful, vengeful critter who never forgets a grudge. Skunk vendettas—who knew? And apparently they are violently opposed to corporal punishment. According to online authorities, sparing the rod is far preferable to riling your skunk with a paddling, no matter how well-deserved it might be.

My wife is an empathic pacifist, a nature lover, a humane human, so phase two of the eradication plan called for baiting two cages with bacon in order to live-trap the stinky-winkies, which then would be relocated.

This is when the trouble began because the traps worked, and the twins caught two skunks in one cage and one in the other. Despite prudently covering the traps—as soon as they picked up the cages, my wife and her sister were both gagged by clouds of skunk spray, and when they set the cages down to seek relief from the gassing, one of the hairy Houdinis somehow escaped. This same stink weasel—whose gang was probably named the Putrid Polecats, the Caustic Kitties, the Pungent Pussies, or if they had a sense of irony, the Nosegays—this same stink weasel appeared at an open window at dinner time and, with fragrant disregard for decorum, blasted away with both anal-gland barrels through the screen, ruining the meal. A sneak attack. Guerilla skunks—what could be more heinous?

My wife said she smelled so bad after this attack that she could smell herself from far away. She said the stench was so inescapable that even her beer tasted skunky. And it didn't work to bathe in tomato juice. (I don't know if she tried the juice from a-Roma tomato.)

The next morning, still reeking, my wife had had enough. She became in-scents-ed and decided to move to Plan B— shooting the skunks. In two days she had gone from empath to sociopath. From ASPCA to NRA. She grabbed shotgun and shells while Sissy loaded the pistol.

The twins were taking no chances: they donned shower caps, dust masks, goggles, latex gloves, ragged shirts, pajama pants, and the cheapest slippers they could find— pink fuzzy ones as it turned out. Then they grabbed their guns and, with the sun directly overhead, stepped outside and took the high ground. Arrayed like an artillery line before them, with untold expertise in chemical warfare and eager to enter the fray—the gang of nine, the Nosegays. The twins knew what had to be done. It was right there staring back at them—in plain black and white. Like a scene out of *Lawrence of Arabia*, my wife, her eyes aglow, began shouting at the top of her lungs, "No prisoners! No prisoners!" And so the battle began.

Never spank your skunk? It's exactly that kind of misguided mollycoddling that's led to rampaging gangs of hoodlum skunks like the ones who harassed and gassed my wife and her sister. So do your duty by society. When your skunk misbehaves, you know what you have to do—spank it!

Watching TV with the Opposite SEX

It's a relaxing evening at home just right for watching a movie. I sit down with my wife on the loveseat and think how nice this is when our cat jumps up between us and my wife announces, "*I'm* picking the movie this time."

I feel it. Something has come between us—besides the cat—and I realize that once again watching a video with my bride is going to be a struggle. Much has been made of the sexes' battle for the remote control, but that's only a small part of the conflict.

My wife's announcement is tantamount to saying, "The movie *you* chose last time stank, so now it's my turn." The principle here, familiar to those who've played pickup basketball, is "make it/take it." You keep the ball until you miss. Apparently my last shot was an airball.

The game rules in my house also include my wife's insistence that the movie can't be very violent. There go *300* and *Dredd* and most of the other films I like. She checks the online motion picture parental guide, which minutely details all violence; degrees, types, and duration of nudity; and exactly how many times and in what context the F-word is used.

Watching TV is even more contentious and perilous for me, and by "TV" I of course mean "transvestites." One source of conflict is that when I watch TV by myself and a commercial comes on, I surf for a backup movie or even two backups so that I always have something interesting on the screen. Supposedly, women are great multitaskers and men are too stupid to do more than one thing at a time, but this claim is not borne out by my wife's and my TV-watching styles. My wife wants the TV left on one channel—even during the 5-minute commercial breaks! On the other hand, I can and do watch 3 different movies sort of simultaneously. I'll be watching *Tootsie*, switch to *Big Momma's House*, and then to *Mrs. Doubtfire*, plus keep up a pop-up-like running commentary of fascinating facts about the movies and actors.

"Do you know who that actor is?"

"No."

"That's Nicholas Hoult. Do you know whom he used to date?"

"No."

"He used to date Jennifer Lawrence. Do you know whom she's dating now?"

"No."

"She's off-and-on seeing Chris Martin, the Coldplay singer, who used to be married to . . . ?"

"I don't know."

"Gwyneth Paltrow, whose mother is . . .?"

Now clearly most women would appreciate my evocative questions and find my abilities impressive, but my wife just thinks I'm annoying. Yes, annoying. I don't know why women think men are annoying when clearly we're *not* annoying, not at all annoying. Annoying?! Geez!

After some of my astute insights, such as "Nobody'd put a laundry basket down on the kitchen table in real life," my wife will ask me, "Why do you always talk to the TV?"

"I wasn't talking to the TV; I was talking to you."

"No you weren't. You were talking to the TV."

"No I wasn't. I was talking to you."

If my trenchant analysis causes my wife to miss some unnecessary dialog on a video, she'll sigh loudly and then replay the last 10 seconds. If it's a TV movie, say the new *Total Recall,* she'll ask in an annoyed tone what the actors said. Of course *I* heard what they said. "That's Kate Beckinsale," I say. "She's been in *Serendipity,* *Underworld,* and *Pearl Harbor,* and she just told Colin Farrell,

I'm not your wife. You just think I am because your brain has been implanted with memories. Actually I'm a secret agent, and my mission is to kill you—or at the very least to stop you from watching 3 channels at once."

Take some advice from me, guys: when you watch TV with the opposite sex, don't expect to be in control. Not even remotely.

Married to an Identical Twin

Carolyn, my significant other, is an identical twin. And while she and her sister are easy to tell apart *now*, that has not always been the case.

Distinguishing which is which in photos before the age of 10 is difficult, and before the age of 5, impossible.

You can imagine how challenging it would have been for their parents to figure out if they were addressing Marilyn or Carolyn. They solved this problem by not even trying. Instead, they just called both girls "Sissy." That way they avoided the embarrassing, inevitable "I'm not Carolyn; I'm Marilyn" response. To this day Carolyn calls Marilyn "Sissy," and Marilyn calls Carolyn "Sissy." When they exchange gifts, all of the tags say, "*To* Sissy. *From* Sissy."

As in Disney movies, the twins took advantage of others' befuddlement. In high school, Carolyn took both her own and Sissy's Latin classes, while in return Sissy doubled up on P.E. classes.

One time, they also exploited their identicalness in the romance department. When they were 15, Marilyn had been ardently hoping for a date with the captain of the football team, and, finally, he called. But Sissy was violently sick with a stomach virus. Determined not to lose her chance, she said "yes" and then began pleading with Carolyn to substitute-date for her. Carolyn raised multiple common-sense objections, but Sissy prevailed. Marilyn assured her, "You don't have to do anything but hold my place. Just be sure to get me a second date. Do whatever it takes to get me a second date." As you might expect, the quarterback, famed for how good he was with his hands, spent all night making passes at Carolyn. Carolyn, for her part, repeatedly deflected them. After his several fumbled attempts, the QB said in exasperation, "You're a lot more shy than I thought you'd be." To which Carolyn replied, "I don't do any of that on a first date." When he asked, "What about a second date?" Carolyn told him encouragingly, "We'll see." The footballer did indeed call again. Marilyn returned early from this second date—looking out of sorts—marched right to Carolyn and said, "Exactly what did you say to him? He was all over me."

Now I know what you're wondering: "Since the twins have a history of being willing and able to impersonate one another, aren't you concerned they might trick *you*?" The answer is "no." These days it's pretty easy to tell them apart . . . unless they're on a car trip together and one of them calls me. You see, they often switch phones. If Carolyn is driving, I know that Sissy might call me on Carolyn's phone, so instead of my usual "Hi, Baby"—I just say "Hi," and if the other person just says "Hi" in response, I keep my words as neutral as possible till I can figure out whether I'm talking to Sissy number one or Sissy number two. I also have to be very careful when Sissy visits because she's always wearing Carolyn's clothes and the twins are of course the same height and body build, so when I'm coming up behind my wife to give her a surprise embrace . . . Well, you get the idea.

Here's the thing: The state of North Carolina, where I reside, sets a lot of store by exactly what's written on birth certificates. And Carolyn and Marilyn's parents couldn't tell them apart—didn't even try to keep straight who was who. So who knows if when the infants learned their names, they learned them correctly? I figure there's a 50-50 chance that the woman I'm married to, who calls herself Carolyn, is actually *legally Marilyn* by birth. And that's how—as far-fetched as it might sound—it's even odds that I'm living in sin, am not actually married to my own wife . . . but instead am legally wedded—to my sister-in-law.

The Identical Twin Defense

One reason that life is so complicated is that not only can lies sometimes sound like the truth but also sometimes the absolute truth can sound like it must be a lie. One example of the latter case was brought home to me because I'm married to an identical twin.

Some years ago, when we were still in the honeymoon phase of our romance, my bride (Carolyn) and I visited her identical twin sister (Marilyn) and her husband in Huntsville, Alabama. Marilyn's husband was a neurosurgeon and the two of them were well-known leading citizens in the community.

I don't know what *your* position is on public displays of affection, but at the time, I was certainly open to them. Thus it was that as we stood waiting in the checkout line at the small Huntsville market closest to my sister-in-law's house, I took advantage of the opportunity to wrap my arms around Carolyn and hold her tight. When we were second in line, the cashier turned to look at us directly. She narrowed her eyes and tilted her head in what seemed to be a look of surprise and disapproval—and she kept staring at us for an uncomfortably long time. I'd never seen her before and thought she must be a serious hater of PDA to be giving us this persistent stink-eye. I gave her a "What's your problem, lady?" look in return, but then my wife, who's always been a lot smarter than I am at analyzing social situations, realized there was more going on here.

One detail I've been saving for you is that Carolyn had a cold and had just the day before developed laryngitis, so when she said to the cashier, "You probably think I'm Marilyn," she said it in a hoarse whisper—(as if she were trying to disguise her voice?) The disapprover slowly nodded her head and drawled, "Mmm hmm." Carolyn then explained, "I'm not Marilyn; I'm her twin sister Carolyn."

The cashier nodded and said, "Mmm hmm" again—but her face said, "So *that's* the way you're going to play this, Marilyn. This is such a lowering of you, to be fooling around with this incredibly good-looking, virile young stud behind your husband's back and then to tell me such an outrageous, bald-faced lie right to my face like I haven't seen you coming in here with your husband for years. Identical twin? Pleeease! Is that really the best lie you can come up with? And the fake voice? That's just insulting."

As you can tell, I'm really good at reading faces.

I don't really remember what Carolyn croaked at her next, but I do remember the stink-eyed cashier kept looking as skeptical and righteously revolted as ever.

After we left the store, my bride sighed and whispered to me, "I think we just got Marilyn in really big trouble. When we get back, we have a *lot* of explaining to do."

Isn't it funny how sometimes the truth doesn't do you any good—unless it is believed?

Dangling in Midair

I watched as two men tied my wife with thick rope, and I watched as she dangled about 40 feet above the ground. Upside down. In public. As others watched.

I'm not sure even the *Kama Sutra* describes anything this kinky.

In case you're wondering, my wife is *not* a circus performer or an aerialist of any kind. At the time of her dangling, she was an English teacher.

Probably, I should back up.

My wife has always been a lot more adventurous than I am, the kind of person who works for Peace Corps in the jungles of South America, or who hikes the coast of the Pacific Northwest on Outward Bound, or who without fear of electrocution installs a dining room dimmer switch.

I know: I'm a lucky man.

So when Carolyn was invited by her students and by an outdoor recreation teacher to go rappelling from the tower at our university, she thought it'd be a hoot. I myself had no wish to die, but I went with her for support—what you might call *ground* support.

So I stood below as Carolyn climbed the ladder to the platform. Then the outdoor rec teacher and an assistant made a rope "seat" for Carolyn, which is a polite way of saying that they made a very tight rope bikini bottom for her. I don't know exactly how to express my feelings as I watched my wife being manhandled in this way. Words fail me. We'd been married over a year, but we'd never done anything *this* intimate.

Finally, Carolyn was ready for the moment of truth. She was tied in and someone was on belay. Holding onto the rope, she stepped off the platform backwards. At which point her head went down, her feet went up, and she was completely vertical, her back flat against the boards. She had a death-grip on the rope.

"Hmm," I thought. "Is that what was supposed to happen?"

Based on Carolyn's frozenness and on the energetic activity of the others on the platform, I could tell it was likely this was *not* what was supposed to happen. Immediately, the outdoor rec teacher lay down on the platform so that his head was just above Carolyn's feet, and I could hear that he was talking to her in low, soothing tones.

Can you imagine how odd it is to watch something like this in silence? I could have yelled out to her, but I had no idea what was going on, and it was clear she needed the help of an expert.

As I learned later, Carolyn's upside-downness was the result of her not being tied correctly. Because of the belay line, she was in no danger of falling, so what the rec teacher was telling her was "Carolyn, you need to let go of the rope. As soon as you do, you'll pop right up and be able to rappel down the face of the tower normally." After a long pause, Carolyn said, "What are my other options? Because there's no way I'm letting go of this rope." And he said, "You *have* to let go of the rope. There are no other options." And she said, "I am not letting go of this rope." And he made his voice as calm and comforting and soothing as possible and said, "Let go, Carolyn. You have to let go."

And I watched as this man, right before God and everybody, tried to seduce my wife: "Let go, Carolyn. Just let go."

He told her, "If you don't let go of the rope, eventually you'll pass out, and then you'll let go, and then you'll pop right up, and everything will be OK. But why not let go now? Trust me."

"I *did* trust you," she said. "And look where it got me."

Did she force her courage to the fore, abandon common sense, and relinquish her grip? Did she hang on until she fainted? Did her husband punch the recreation teacher in the face?

I'm gonna leave you dangling.

Best Friends & Wives

My wife is my best friend. Am I an idiot or what?

I do realize how wonderfully romantic it might sound to say, "My wife/husband/partner is also my best friend," but really it's a very bad idea.

Recently, my wife spent two weeks with her sister and then shortly afterward left for four days to take a shoe-making class. All I had for company was a not-too-intelligent cat. I had no best friend to kill time with. Nobody I could call to go bowling, or hiking, or to get tacos, or to play Pandemic. This is just one reason you never want your best friend to be your better half.

Suppose you want to go out to a restaurant. Ordinarily if you go out to eat with a friend and suggest Dutch Treat, your etiquette is impeccable. But if you're with your wife and when the check comes you start figuring out, "Let's see: you had the two glasses of wine and you ate, I'd say, about ⅔ of the appetizers . . . ," everybody looks at you like you're a cheap bastard.

And another thing: Imagine having to admit to people, "I've been sleeping with my best friend. For *years*." You wouldn't even be able to say, "We didn't plan it; it just happened." No you'd have to admit, "We *planned* to sleep together—from the very start."

All *kinds* of absurd predicaments can arise. If my wife ever throws me out of the house, right after the door slams I'll be in the weird position of having to turn around to knock on the door, and when she opens it (if I'm lucky), I'll have to say, "Carolyn just threw me out. Can I sleep on your couch until she takes me back?"

And if she contemplates divorcing me, what then? *She's* the one I'll have to call up for comfort and advice. She'll have to listen for hours as I paddle around in a pool of self-pity because, as my best friend, that's what she signed up for. Do you think that when I complain about my wife, I can count on her to tell me, "I never liked her" or "You're too good for her anyway"? If she refuses to listen, if she blows me off, then she'll be in breach of the best-friend contract, and it'll all be over.

Think about how desperate your situation will be if your wife is divorcing you *and* your best friend simultaneously dumps you. You'll be so needy you'll be like a mangy, listless, ill-tempered tomcat that's been returned to the shelter. How easy do you think it's going to be to get adopted when your file reads, "Eats too much, sheds badly, yowls all night, and as for the litter box, he misses about half the time. Honestly, I think he's *trying* to miss. And he expects *me* to clean up after him."

I hope I've made my point, but in case I haven't, I'm going to ask my wife to critique this, and in case she's afraid to be totally honest, I'm then going to ask for feedback from my very best friend.

In-Tents Camping: Be Prepared

When my stepson came home from school one day all excited about joining Cub Scouts, I didn't realize how my life was about to change. My wife, an actual blood-relative to my stepson, refused to go to the interest meeting, citing that she had been a Cubmaster before and had already learned her lesson under absurd circumstances I'm not at liberty to divulge. "Besides, this will be a good way for you and Farzad to bond," she suggested. So I naively agreed to go. "You probably shouldn't mention my name," she said as I was leaving. I didn't realize the main point of an interest meeting is to pressure parents into agreeing to be Scout Leaders. I'm proud to say I steadfastly resisted and didn't volunteer. I was overworked and underqualified, having never myself progressed beyond Tenderfoot. Yes, I held out for almost a month before agreeing to be Assistant Cubmaster "on paper." I wouldn't really have to do anything, I was assured.

While still Webelos, my stepson and his pack were invited as guests by local Boy Scout Troop 420 on their first campout late one October, and I agreed to tag along. The Scout motto is "Be Prepared!" But nothing, I mean nothing, prepares you for weekends in the woods with adolescent boys. (Think *Lord of the Flies* or *Hunger Games*.) A Scout leader explained we'd be at Camp Runamoka, a permanent Boy Scout camp with cabins containing bunk beds, and our hosts would cook for us.

The Scout Law notwithstanding, this BS leader proved not to be Trustworthy. First, the "cabin" walls were solid only halfway up. The other half was screening. It was a c-cold and brr-breezy night inside as well as out. There were indeed bunkbeds, but the stains and hammock-like sags of the mattresses suggested WW I vintage. Secondly, we learned after arriving that our meals were *not* going to be provided. So off we went to the nearest grocery store for hotdogs, chips, and marshmallows.

Anyone who's ever camped with young boys I'm sure cringed at the word "marshmallows." But this was my first time. The boys delighted in setting the puffy confections on fire, then running around with their sticks ablaze. The flaming marshmallows of course turned black, melted, and fell off the sticks so that soon our campground was a sticky minefield, and shortly after that everyone's shoes were afflicted with hideous gobs of goo, and then the cabin floors, and then everything sitting on the floors was ruined. A Scout is Clean. A Scout is Thrifty.

Two other campouts stand out, both cancelled in progress because of weather. The first was cut short by gale-force winds and the threat of hail and tornadoes. My nylon pop-tent contracted so violently it looked like an accordion. Two Scouts—whose parents, suspiciously, did not answer their phones—spent the night on my living room floor. And then there was the deluge campout when it simply wouldn't stop raining. By the time the Scoutmaster had had enough, the field around our cars was flooded, and we spent an hour pushing our cars out of a mud pit. I actually got splattered all over from the spinning rear wheels of a car I was pushing and arrived home looking like Schwarzenegger near the end of *Predator*.

The main attraction of Scouting for me was the opportunity to share activities with my stepson. But I was involved for so many years that eventually I was asked to help with our troop's week-long summer camp even though Farzad was with his father a thousand miles away. That summer our troop shared a campsite with another troop, and at one point the other troop's leader informed me, a stranger to him, that he was leaving to get hamburgers from McDonald's, and he indicated he was sure his charges would be fine unsupervised. During this interim his boys got some valuable experience creating an explosive homemade torch from a hairspray can. A Boy Scout is Brave.

When my Scout Leader relief showed up and asked what I liked best about the summer camp experience, I said, "The meals." When I asked her what she liked best, she said, "I like helping young men get a solid start on achieving their full potential in life." What a great answer. Boy, did I feel like a heel: small, petty, inadequate, and embarrassed. After I heard her much better answer, I thought to myself, "For me it's still the meals."

No, I wasn't prepared, wasn't qualified. I wasn't even Cheerful. But I did go. I was Loyal and maybe Helpful. And I survived enough campouts and enough meetings, banquets, and boards of review to see my stepson advance from Bear Cub to Eagle Scout.

And it was worth it.

Ghosts of Christmas Past

My wife refuses to let me be the one to put lights on our Christmas tree each year. She says I'm still too haunted by my father's traditions even though my father has not walked the earth for lo these 30 years. My father loved a big and therefore heavy Christmas tree. This isn't a problem for most people. They cut off the lower branches, stick the tree firmly down into the bottom of a heavy-duty stand, tighten the screws and presto, a stable tree. But my father insisted on saving the lower branches. Fir branches all the way down to the floor were to him the Mona Lisa that he strove to paint each Yuletide. But these same gorgeous branches prevented the trunk from reaching the bottom of the stand. So each December my father's four sons began a search in the scrap lumber pile, the toy box, and the garage for the exact combination of wood blocks and shims to fill the gap between trunk and stand. This was not an easy mission, and each failed attempt unleashed a barrage of my father's cursing that I still associate with Christmas to this day. Presents, special foods, cold weather, carols, and Christmas cursing. Most memorably, one year the perfect last piece of my father's Jenga shim tower turned out to be a rusty axe head. Not surprisingly, this particular tree fell over the next day and then a second time the day after that. But my father still protected his masterpiece. A little fishing line from tree top to a hook newly screwed into the wall and voilà—low branches *and* stability.

My mother, for her part, had a holiday gift for pushing herself past the point of exhaustion, and it was a point of pride for her to be so exhausted on Christmas day that she would usually collapse by early afternoon, just after preparing her usual sumptuous Christmas dinner feast. My mother saw Christmas as something she—and she alone—

had to "put together," as if it were a child's cardboard play set with 300 tabs needing to be fitted into 300 slots. At Thanksgiving she'd say, "Here it is almost December, and I've hardly begun putting Christmas together." About two weeks before C-Day, she'd nearly be in tears lamenting, "I just don't see how I'm going to put Christmas together this year." She always wanted to give perfect gifts, which she envisioned as not only something the recipient really wanted but also as something that would be a big surprise, preferably an outrageous surprise. Despite this emphasis on surprise, she always asked me what I wanted. I remember one exchange when I was in my forties, and my mother was in her seventies.

Mother: I was thinking that for Christmas you might like something for your garden. How about a gazing ball or a light-up garden gnome?

Me: No thank you. I don't really like man-made stuff in my garden. I love flowers and flowering trees. I've been wanting a weeping cherry tree.

Mother: How would I get that to you?

Me: The nursery here has some. You could just give me the money and I'll go get one.

Mother: That's no fun.

Me: So you want it to be something fun for you to give?

Mother: No, I want you to get what you want.

Me: I'd love the money for a weeping cherry tree.

Mother: How about a nice gazing ball?

My mother loved little children, and she never admitted to herself that her sons grew up. One Christmas when I was ten, I enjoyed playing with a paddle ball toy I had received in my stocking. So my mother continued giving me a Bo-Lo or Fli-Back paddle ball every Christmas until I was well into my thirties. And even after all of us were grown, my mother continued to *hide* our Christmas gifts so our little-boy surprise would not be spoiled when we visited her in December. As a result, she spent a lot of time the last week before Christmas in frustration and panic trying to find gifts she knew she'd purchased. What she had so carefully "put together" was once again falling apart.

Our traditions did not entirely ignore the true meaning of Christmas. One year, father and sons nailed together a crude four-poster stable frame. The foldable metal legs of a TV tray stand and a couple of rectangles of thin plywood served as the manger. We spread brown pine straw on top of the stable and also used it to pad the manger, bought a couple of feet of burlap for swaddling clothes, and lit the scene with a staked blue floodlight. All we needed was a baby Jesus, which we began an earnest search for. No stuffed plush animal seemed suitable, but we finally found a no-longer-used doll—a foot-long plastic Dennis the Menace doll with a hole in one toe and with bright yellow paint over wavy ridges on his head serving as hair, "hair" which included a large hooked cowlick. Surely at one time Dennis had had clothes, but by the time we pressed him into service as our holiday-display messiah, he was an eyeful of pink plastic nakedness. But, then, once we swaddled his body, who would ever know? Except for that head. Our golden-haired, cowlicked, freckle-faced Jesus.

All of my mother's decorating, elaborate gift-wrapping, and special-food cooking led inevitably to another Spencer childhood Christmas tradition—what my father called the Merry Christmas Garbage Parade. The volume of our holiday garbage vastly overwhelmed our garbage-can capacity, so we would gather up a metaphorical parade of trash-filled bags and boxes and set out like magi on an unwise and illegal quest bearing "gifts" for an out-of-the-way, unwatched dumpster behind a shopping center or school. I was otherwise quite law-abiding, so these journeys always filled me with the excited fear of being caught by the authorities. To this day, nothing brings back my childhood spirit of Christmas so much as the stealthy commission of misdemeanor. And, really, how else am I going to be able to dispose of an oversized garish garden gnome?

So, yes, I'm still haunted by ghosts of Christmases Past—by images of maternal excess and exhaustion, by memories of Christmas cursing and petit crime—but my parents loved Christmas in their own ways and loved their sons. Their spirits will always be their gift to me, will always be a part of my Christmas Present.

My Father's Sense of Humor

When my wife tells me, "You're not as funny as you think," I freely own up to my failings and admit, "That's my dad's fault." Yes, the nut doesn't fall far from the tree, so if I'm not funny, it's because for over thirty years I drank from the fountain of my father's sense of humor.

He loved puns. He used to send me headlines he clipped from newspapers: "Bill's Chances Getting Slimmer by the Minute" (meaning *me*); "Hooker Seeks Help on Island Project" ("Hooker," here, a man's name); and from the newspaper's TV guide section "*The Houston Knights*: Good Ol' Boy, Chicago Detective Born to Butt Heads" (which my father knew I'd read as "Born to Buttheads"). I once gave him a *Humor in the Headlines* book filled with such double entendres, and he read them out loud to me and got so tickled he started laughing uncontrollably to the point of giggling in tears. He couldn't stop, and I began to fear for his health. After two days of nonstop laughter, I hid the book where he couldn't find it.

My father also admired irony, understatement, and exaggeration, and sometimes employed these techniques in uncomfortable ways. Once after he sent me into a McDonald's for a take-out order, the service was slow, and he came in after five minutes and announced for everyone to hear, "I just came in to see if you'd decided to camp out here tonight." Hearkening back to his military service, he called day-long odious work projects "GI parties," and he "invited" me and my brothers to them.

Dad also enjoyed insult humor and plagiarized examples of it from literature. When he thought I was slow completing an errand, he'd ask, "How did you travel? By ox cart?" (from the play *The Man Who Came to Dinner*). And when he was invited to attend some event of dubious desirability, he'd say, "I'll go—if a lunch is provided" (from Dickens, regarding Scrooge's funeral).

My father's sense of humor also embraced the dark. His favorite *New Yorker* cartoon was of a woman running along the beach, the shadow of an overhead pterodactyl with a man dangling in its talons just ahead of her, with the caption "The keys, George. Drop the keys!" This caption was his refrain whenever he was struck by gallows humor. He celebrated my mother's frequent mid-year firings of incompetent teachers at her private school each time with another refrain: "Merry Christmas and goodbye." He intimated that the "Merry Christmas" would be a nice, softening touch to the firing. And once when he was in the courthouse as city attorney in charge of acquiring land for a new road right of way and a street evangelist accosted him in the hallway with "Brother, are you headed to heaven?" my father shot back, "No, in fact, Brother, I'm headed to a condemnation."

The morning after my father died, the whole family had gathered at the kitchen table when the phone rang. My sister-in-law answered it and began a tangle with a persistent solicitor. We could see in her face and hear in her voice her increasing discomfort as we listened to her side of the exchange:

> He's not here right now. . . .
> No, that wouldn't be a good time to call back. . . .
> No, that wouldn't be a good time either. . . .
> There's not really *any* good time. . . .
> I'm sorry. The truth is he just died.

At the table we began snickering with the first "He's not here right now" and laughed harder and louder the deeper my sister-in-law dug into her grave predicament. I feel sure my father would have forgiven us. In fact, I think he actually would've liked it that we celebrated his life, celebrated his sense of humor—by inappropriately, unreservedly laughing our heads off.

After all, we learned it from him.

Daddy vs. the Smoke Alarm

My father, usually a reasonable man, had an uneasy relationship with inanimate objects that crossed him. Once after banging his head on a car door frame, he beat the top of the car repeatedly with the side of his fist. His car must've gotten the message because the door frame never attacked him again. Another time when he was opening a beach umbrella and pinched his hand, he threw the umbrella down and cursed it in waves till the tide turned. But his greatest victory was his battle with a hotel smoke alarm. I can tell you the story now because I'm almost sure the statute of limitations has run out.

My father, mother, one brother and I were on a vacation to Epcot. Daddy had found bargain-price accommodations in Orlando in a brand new condominium building that was functioning as a hotel until more units could be sold. The condo was pristine, still smelling of carpet glue, and spread around our entire suite were placards warning of how hypersensitive the building's fire alarm system was. The slightest whiff of burnt toast could set it off, and God forbid anyone should light a cigarette in the room.

All these warnings with their earnest, exclamatory tone freaked my father out because, you see, my mother was a devoted smoker. If there had been an NSRA, a National Smokers' Rights Association, my mother would have been president. But at my father's insistence she grudgingly promised not to smoke inside unless it was directly under the vent hood fan.

At about 4:30 in the morning, I was waked up—we all were—by the blaring of an alarm. In seconds we were standing under the smoke alarm in a panic. My father stood on a kitchen chair to look for an off switch but couldn't find one. He pried off the cover to remove the batteries, but there weren't any; the alarm was wired into the electrical system. I was sure that any second irate neighbors would be pounding on our door to complain about the sleep-killing siren in our room, but there seemed to be no way to safely disconnect the relentless horn above our heads.

That's when my father's years of training in hand-to-hand combat with unruly objects kicked in. He started smashing the guts of our smoke alarm with his fist. He meant to make it shut up even if he had to kill it. Soon it was a blood-stained pulp of aluminum and electronics. There was no way it could still be functioning—and yet the siren screamed steadily as ever.

Not until that moment did it occur to me that the source of ear-splitting noise might be somewhere other than inside our unit. I opened the door to the hall to even more decibels and realized at once that the sound was coming from a fire alarm horn in the hallway.

I should say at this point that in general I'm a mostly honest person who in principle favors the truth over lying, but what happened next enlightened me to how people can make up outrageous lies and then stick to them no matter what.

By the time the firemen knocked on our door, my father had already replaced the smoke alarm cover, and we had moved the chair back to the kitchen. The firefighters explained that there was no fire and that the building's computerized system analytics flagged only a malfunctioning smoke detector in our unit. "Hunh," my father said. They removed the cover and stared at the destruction and blood. Though my father did the best he could at hiding his injuries, he literally had blood on his hand. He was literally red-handed. Even so, I realized that there was no way we could voluntarily admit that based on mistaken assumptions, my father had smashed and smashed the ever-lovin' hell out of our smoke alarm. So we stood there silently, complicitly, nervously, trying to look as innocent as possible.

When the fire chief concluded that the previous occupants must've damaged the detector and not reported it, we nodded to imply our agreement as well as our sad condemnation of people who could so wantonly destroy such an important safety device without even having the decency to own up to it.

That was the last time I know of that my father engaged in violent conflict with adversarial things. He had murdered an innocent hotel smoke alarm—and had gotten away with it. And I think word got around.

The Root of All My Imperfections

I had a difficult childhood. Both of my parents were addicts, and my three brothers and I suffered the consequences. My parents were addicted to nicotine. Yes, my mother and father went around all day with butts in their mouths.

Both were chain smokers, and the word "chain" is especially apt since it conveys not only the literal truth that they smoked one cigarette right after the other but also the metaphorical truth that they were in bondage, shackled to the demon weed. Since they smoked cigarettes high in tar content, you might say they were tarred and fettered.

Roofers could have repaired leaks with the tar in their lungs. The DOT could have paved potholes.

Like every other child of a smoker parent, what I dreaded most was the long car trip during hot weather. My father insisted that whenever the car's air conditioner was running, all windows had to be tightly closed. But with 2 chain smokers and 4 boys in a tightly closed car, the oxygen soon began to run out. So when I started getting light-headed, I would sneak down my window only an inch or so and put my nose directly in the path of the stream of fresh air. I usually got about 5 minutes before my father found me out and commanded me to eliminate my oxygen supply. "Sure, Daddy. No problem. I'll just hold my breath." I wonder why my father's brain was so *clouded*.

Barbecuers smoke meat to preserve it. I figure based on 20 years of being smoked, I should live to be a hundred.

On cool-weather car trips, we were allowed to have the windows down, but these excursions had their own lookouts. Usually, my parents' exhalations would be sucked out the front windows and then sucked *into* the back seat, so their smoke was being blasted into our faces at about 55 miles per hour. Once, a cinder from my father's flicked cigarette jetted in through my window, zeroed in on my face, and lodged in my left nostril. That's absolutely true.

They say that smoking stunts your growth. Both of my parents smoked at least 3 packs a day, which means I was getting the benefits of 6 packs a day. If not for all that smoke, I would've been at least 6'5". I could've played in the NBA, dated tall models, and looked down on my friends—except for the devil's chimneys my parents kept lit in their mouths.

And I'm sure it's not just my height that was affected. Back in 1957 when my mother was pregnant with me, doctors didn't yet know the dangers, so I'm sure Momma kept puffing away, hence all my imperfections: my flaws, my failings, my inadequacies, my crowded lower teeth, my overly manly nose, my excessive punning. Thanks a lot, Momma.

I think you can understand why even to this day I still feel resentment, resentment that lingers in the air like—like—like thick, lazily curling, acrid, carcinogenic smoke.

But for the noxious weed, I could've been George Clooney.

A Mother's High-Calorie Love

My mother equated food with love and food that she cooked for her children with mother's love. The more food, the more calories, the more trouble, the more time involved, the more pans used, the bigger mess made—the more love. So my mother's love was messy, exhausting, and fattening.

All four of my mother's sons have had weight issues. Most of the time I've been the leanest son since I periodically swear off sweets. I go on the wagon because I'm addicted to sugar. Just a few sweets crank up my sugar craving and I return to obsessively thinking about cookies, pies, pecan twirls, honey buns, and brown sugar cinnamon Pop-Tarts. I also have an itchy-rash dairy allergy, which further stymied my mother. "Can you have eggs?" my mother asked nearly every visit. "Yes," I'd say, "as long as it doesn't come from a cow's udder, I can have it, and cows don't lay eggs." Repeatedly, my mother fretted, "I wish I could figure out some dessert I could make for you." Some years ago she made me Shoo-Fly pie and was proud that it contained "no sugar." When I pointed out the cups of Karo syrup and molasses ingredients, she saw no connection and assured me that she had made it before for her diabetic neighbor. Another time when she was making my favorite supper—fried chicken—she delighted in telling me that she had taken the trouble to soak the chicken all afternoon in milk. When I searched her face for signs she was joking, I found none.

My brothers and I and our wives constantly fought to make my mother's cooking life easier, but we failed. One brother bought her a microwave oven, which she refused to use even once during the twenty years she owned it. I praised her the first time she bought an already-cooked rotisserie chicken, but then she baked it at 350 degrees for an additional hour in her own oven in her own pan. It would have been juicier served directly from Piggly Wiggly, but what's juicy Piggly Wiggly love compared to mother's love no matter how dried up?

She refused to ever serve or eat leftovers (Who wants leftover love?) and she despised casseroles, possibly because they could be entirely made and served in just one dish. Early on, we all gave up trying to make cooking supper easier for her, but I drew the battle line at lunches. My usual cold-cut sandwich and chips required only one paper plate and one knife. But my mother always wanted to cook something: BLTs, grilled cheese sandwiches, or her takes-all-day homemade vegetable soup. I was sure I had outflanked her once when I told her, "All I want is a peanut butter and jelly sandwich." Five minutes later when I entered the kitchen, there she stood awkwardly holding a mixing bowl, desperately struggling to stir together the jelly and stiffened-because-refrigerated peanut butter. I had lost the battle.

Another time she proudly showed me the small handful of tiny, tiny peas she'd gotten from an hour's work shelling snow peas. We had lost the war.

My mother equated eating what she cooked with accepting her love, and that's why I was her most problematic son. She was happiest when the massive amounts of food she cooked for a family feast were completely consumed, and she noted who ate how many helpings. She would tell me, "Kelly had three helpings of my spaghetti; did you see?"—offering Kelly to me as a good example, an enviable role model. Many years ago, with a large spoonful of mashed potatoes poised over my plate, she asked, "Would you like some more?" A second after I said, "No thank you," plop went the potatoes onto my plate.

Despite my efforts to view my mother's philosophy about cooking and eating with a certain detached sense of humor, I guess the nut doesn't fall far from the tree. While she was under Hospice care, I and her other caregivers devoted a lot of energy to demonstrating our love to her through food. I'm convinced that love—in the form of cheesy grits, homemade chicken and rice soup, and other tasty offerings—is what kept her alive eight months longer than anyone expected. And I found myself becoming competitive. After I heard that my sister-in-law Pam was "such a good cook" for the tenth time, I upped my game: made blueberry muffins, baked apple pies with apples from my own tree, grilled steaks and zucchini squash, learned how to cook two of her favorite tricky dishes—cornbread hoecakes and fried eggplant. ("I'll be damned if Pam loves her more than I do.")

I no longer dismiss my mother's ideas about hands-on homemade nourishment. Ever since she died, I've been losing weight. My mother's love is slowly melting away.

I have an image of my mother in my mind that I think will always stick with me. She's standing in her kitchen, where flour, sugar, Karo syrup, and bacon grease have exploded all over the counters and the floor. Dirty pans, bowls, and utensils are scattered everywhere like shrapnel. She stands amidst this domestic war zone smiling an exhausted smile, an ounce of tiny peas in one hand and a big pot of mother's love boiling over on the stove.

Bill Spencer

Dying to Have a Clean Garage

Lots of people have two-car garages. My mother had a two-*couch* garage: two couches, a gigantic conference table, three bookcases with books, three living room chairs, a rocking chair, a coffee table, a desk, a cedar hope chest containing her wedding dress and her wedding cake topper, about 50 loaded moving boxes, and about 50 junk-filled garbage bags. That's what I said, garbage bags. (Picture the garbage-strike airport scene in *The Fifth Element*.)

Yes, the garage in the last house my mother lived in was a remarkable mess for twenty years despite the fact that I and others worked to clear it out—for twenty years.

My mother never wanted to throw anything away since she might need it later. I'd ask, "May I throw out this old pocketbook? It's mildewed and the clasp is broken." She'd say, "Why do you always want to get rid of my nice things?"

My mother's garage was huge—larger than needed for two SUV's—but most of the twenty years she owned it, only two narrow paths through the tall forest of boxes and bags were navigable.

"I'm going to clean out that garage one of these days," I heard my mother say dozens of times. When I offered to deal with the boxes and bags, she said, "No, nah anh. I need to sort everything myself so you don't throw away something I might need." When I asked her if she wanted to go through a bag or two with my help, she'd say, "Not today. You're only home for a short time, and I don't want you working the whole time. What would you like to do for fun?"

After a couple of years of this same scene playing over and over, I became a ninja trash assassin. With the theme music to *Mission Impossible* humming in my head, I began stealthily going through boxes and bags when my mother was asleep, or watching TV, or reading a book. Often she'd ask, "What have you been doing?" and I'd say, "Just walking around," or "I've been resting in the rocking chair." "You're not working in the garage, are you?" she'd ask. "No, of course not," I reassured her. "I'm having fun."

Many times I would sneak a junk bag back to my guest bedroom and sort through it late at night or early in the morning with the door closed. After checking that the coast was clear, I'd tiptoe out to the outside garbage bin with all the trash; then little by little I'd furtively ferry what was worth saving to its rightful place. Mission accomplished. One down. Only 49 to go.

I should explain about the bags. Whenever guests were expected, my mother would rake everything she'd piled on the top of her kitchen table into a 13-gallon white trash bag and take it out to the garage. Each bag contained all types of paper goods, unused but ruined by being bent, wrinkled, and roach-stained: typing paper, stationery, all sizes of envelopes, file folders (to help her get organized), and unsent special occasion cards. Each bag also held catalogs, newspapers, unopened junk mail, many letters (since she saved every one of the hundreds she received), photographs, bills (both paid and unpaid), payment notices from Medicare and Blue Cross, outdated bank statements, old grocery lists, filled-out but unsent order forms, a few paperback romance novels, a partly filled out crossword puzzle book, one or two Scotch tape dispensers, 5-10 Hall's mentholyptus lozenges, at least one disposable lighter, matches, loose cigarettes, 3-4 used emery boards, bobby pins, pencils, leaky pens, dried-up magic markers, change worth $1-3, sometimes currency, and always a seemingly endless flow of individual plastic vials of artificial tears.

Have you ever noticed that if you add a "b" (for "bags") to the middle of "garage" it spells "garbage"?

Occasionally, a bag had a torn scrap of paper taped to it with a note in my mother's handwriting that said, "Needs to be sorted." That always made me laugh.

The last time I saw my mother's garage was three months after she died. It was completely clear—well, almost. There was just one roll of leftover carpeting. My oldest brother asked me if we should discard it or save it for the next tenants. I didn't hesitate. "Let's toss it," I said. "Mother wanted a cleared garage for 20 years—so I think she'd call us on the carpet. Let's get rid of this last remnant."

I hope my mother knows she finally got her wish.

Thanksgiving Fare is Fowl

Thanksgiving is a time for family. Not just your familiar family but also your spouse's family. Your spouse's strange, weird family.

One Thanksgiving that we spent at my in-laws' is one I won't forget.

Soon after we arrived on Wednesday, my wife's parents offered to show us the turkey that would be the centerpiece of our next-day's feast. I expected to be ushered over to the refrigerator, but instead I was led outside onto the screened porch. "We read an article about thawing the turkey on a porch so it doesn't take up all the room in the refrigerator."

"Wow, Phyllis. How resourceful. How long has it been out here?"

"Oh, a few days."

I noticed that the porch wasn't very cool. In fact, I thought it was kind of warmish. The screening had been lined with thick plastic, and I also noticed a running space heater. "What's the heater for?" I asked.

"That's so the plants don't get cold."

Then I was shown the turkey. My eyes widened, and I shot my wife a sideways glance. Here on an uncovered platter was the inside-side of a sawed-in-half raw turkey: smooth-cut bones and smooth-cut cartilage—a cross-section view of a turkey's skeletal structure like you'd expect from a biology-class turkey anatomy lesson. It was not appetizing. And I wondered, "How can you stuff half a turkey?" My father-in-law proudly explained, "We're saving the other half for Christmas. I cut it with my table saw."

"Wow, Bob," I said. "Who knew your woodworking skills would come in so handy for food preparation?"

My wife gently pointed out the health danger and repeatedly tried to persuade her parents to move the mutilated carcass to more trustworthy refrigeration but with no luck.

The next day at dinner, our table was far from traditional. The sitting-up, symmetrical, whole, perky turkey was absent from our tableau. Our dissected half-bird lay on its side—as if it had been brutally murdered. Our table was certainly no Norman Rockwell painting. No, not Norman Rockwell. More like Norman Bates.

And when Dad-in-Law raised the knife above his head and began stabbing (I mean carving) the fowl thing in front of us, the social awkwardness reached its peak, for my wife and I had decided we would avoid eating even the smallest bit of what surely had to be food-poisoning flesh. This would be a totally turkey-less Thanksgiving, but there was no way I was going to risk spending the rest of the holiday in the bathroom with Sam & Ella.

"I'll just have a small piece to start," I said. "The smaller the better," I thought since I had to hide it under the other food on my plate. I had to make some pretense of eating it, so I cut it up into ever-smaller chunks and secreted these under the lettuce in my salad.

Meanwhile, my in-laws were stuffing themselves with what I was sure would necessitate a Thanksgiving-afternoon race to the Emergency Room.

After dinner, my wife and I watched our hosts with intense suspense and scrutiny, but the expected debacle of digestion never materialized. "How can this be?" I wondered, and then I remembered the scientific studies being conducted on vultures to discover why they don't get sick from eating spoiled carrion. Obviously, these studies should have been expanded to include my in-laws.

Thanksgiving is about family and giving thanks, so I distracted myself from my hunger that afternoon by counting my blessings. "Dear Lord, thank you that I did not ridiculously overeat this Thanksgiving; thank you that I escaped the misery of food poisoning; and thank you most of all that despite being raised by two such odd parents, my wife turned out (relatively) normal." Yes, I truly had much to be thankful for.

Especially that we'd already decided to spend Christmas—thank goodness—at home.

Home-Cooked Turkey

When I walked in the door, my heart fell into my stomach. Not literally. That would be a condition known technically in medical circles as "death." I wasn't dead; I was just dying inside. Again, not literally.

It was almost noon Thanksgiving morning, and my wife and I had just walked into her parents' house. This late, and I didn't smell even the faintest hint of roasting turkey, one of my favorite aromas in the world, and I thought, "Uh oh, we're in trouble. Turkey trouble."

My wife's relationship to her parents was storied and precarious, so we were not on the sort of terms where we could ask, "What are we doing about the Thanksgiving dinner you invited us for, that we drove all morning from another state for?"

And they didn't volunteer any information about meal plans either.

I began to wish I hadn't skipped breakfast to leave room for the huge anticipated feast.

About 2:00 my in-laws indicated we were going for a drive. There was no mention of food, no reference to dinner whatsoever. They drove us around town for nearly an hour. Literally. At one point, they drove us all the way around a large nursing home building. Drove very slowly and interestedly, and I thought, "Oh my God, is *this* where they're taking us to eat?" But then we drove away, and I exhaled in relief.

OK, so this year there would be no home-cooked turkey for me. "It's not the end of the world," I said to myself. Maybe they're taking us to a nice restaurant. But, no, they were not taking us to a nice restaurant. Maybe they're taking us to a medium-level chain restaurant, say an Applebee's or a Ruby Tuesday's. No, not that either. Just before 3:00, my father-in-law drove back to the nursing home that we had circled earlier, and this time—he parked. We were going to have Thanksgiving dinner at a nursing home that had opened up its dining room to the public for the holiday. An assisted living facility, an institution for those of an advanced age, a home for old folks. From a certain point of view, I was going to get what I expected—a home-cooked meal; I just hadn't expected it to be a *nursing*-home-cooked meal.

Why had we driven around the building earlier? I never did figure that out.

To be fair, the nursing home dining room was probably, under usual circumstances, an attractive one, even having a double fireplace in the center of the large room. But these were not usual circumstances. My guess is that there had been hourly shifts beginning at 11:00 a.m., which would mean we were there for the fifth shift. There were signs everywhere of an overwhelmed, exhausted staff. Many empty tables were still covered in what looked like battle carnage. Bits of uncleared turkey carcass and spatters of gelatinous cranberries all around us. Most of the tables remained uncleared during our entire delightful stay.

Only fifteen minutes after we sat down, our waiter appeared and took our drink orders. We never saw him again. We never saw *any* waiter again until about twenty minutes later, after Dad-in-law went to see what had happened. Apparently, our first waiter's shift had ended, and he had failed to pass us on to anyone else.

At 4:10, just as I was fainting, the food arrived. My first food of the day. It was OK—for cold, dry institutional food—but of course there'd be no leftovers, no turkey sandwiches that night, no heated-up stuffing. In fact, *no* food was offered that night. Why should there be any supper when we hadn't finished dinner until 4:30?

That night, as my stomach grumbled, I counted my blessings. I gave thanks for the wonderful opportunity to work on my food addiction. Gave thanks that my wife is so much more holiday-oriented than her parents. And I even thought my way through my disappointment over not having what I considered a traditional Thanksgiving. I re-envisioned the experience. I came to think of it as Thanksgiving at Grandma's house. Only in this case—two hundred grandmas' house.

What could be more traditional than that?

The OLD Neighborhood

I've been to paradise. And it was hell.

My wife's parents for a time lived in a carefully designed Tennessee retirement community that I'll call Ideal Meadow Cove, and at the start of my first visit there I was struck by its idyllic perfection. All the houses were constructed of matching stained wood and stone and were set on wooded lots near golf courses and a beautiful lake. The small lawns were impeccably manicured; flowers bloomed everywhere; there was no litter—in fact no eyesores of any kind; and it was truly peaceful and quiet.

It was without a doubt the creepiest experience of my life. All the houses were new. All the roads were new. *Every*thing was new. Except the people. The people were old.

I soon learned that the ostensible perfection had been achieved only at the cost of a diabolical level of control by the real estate company that owned this community. After my in-laws bought their lot, they had only three basic house plans to choose from. Lawns were *required* to be kept mowed. If the grass grew higher than the allowed number of inches, company mowers were dispatched and the homeowners were charged and fined. My in-laws could have no outdoor pets, no vegetable gardens in the yard, and there were regulations about the duration and noise-level of visits from young grandchildren.

When my wife and I accompanied her parents to church, I was astonished. I know that many churches have elders. But this congregation had ONLY elders. As for their hair, there must have been 50 shades of gray. The Bible reading was naturally from the OLD Testament—something concerning Methusaleh if I remember correctly. The hymns were "That OLD-time Religion" and "The OLD Rugged Cross."

After church I went with my father-in-law to see one of his neighbors in this Garden of Eden. The neighbor was in a wheelchair, and strapped to his face he had an oxygen tube that serpentined for at least 50 feet in coils throughout the house. The house had a close view of the lake but an even closer view of eternity.

After only a few years, my in-laws left Ideal Meadow Cove, moved to Alabama to a neighborhood without restrictions, with a noisy Interstate less than a mile away, with a trailer two lots down, with campers and fishing boats parked in the weedy, dirt-patched front yards nearby. Where funerals were not the only events they were ever invited to. Where my father-in-law had a huge garden filled with the fruits of the field.

And a blueberry bush, from which he picked a handful of ripe berries, took them to his mate, and offered her to eat.

Learnin'

Sister Mary Barbarian

My ninth-grade English teacher was named Sister Mary Barbara, but for purposes of anonymity, I'll call her Sister Mary Barbarian. She was the toughest, strictest, unyieldingest teacher I ever had—a member of the order the Sisters of *Mercy*. Who says nuns don't have a sense of humor?

Sr. Barbara taught me my freshman year at a Catholic high school—Mount de Sales—in Room 3 of a building named *Mercy* Hall. Who says nuns don't have an incredible sense of humor?

I was a straight-A student and was used to being the teacher's pet. Sr. Barbara didn't have pets. The first time I raised my hand to volunteer an answer in her class, she narrowed her eyes at me and ordered, "Put your hand down." Then she said, "If I want you to answer a question, I'll call on you." Another time she yelled at me when I glanced at the clock at the back of the room. "Don't you turn your head. I'll let you know when the class is over," she said. Various classmates provoked her ire and incurred her caustic tongue for such egregious misconduct as yawning, coughing, sneezing, hiccupping, and audibly exhaling. Yes, exhaling. Sr. B warned the student who exhaled, "Nobody gets that relaxed in MH 3." I have to confess she was right about that. Nobody did get that relaxed in MH 3. And I'll say this for Sr. Barbara's tactics: when you get jumped on for breathing, you don't dare contemplate any actual misbehavior.

I wonder if HBO would be interested in a script for a World War II-type movie entitled *Escape from MH 3*?

Sr. Barbara gave us hours of homework every night in literature, grammar, and vocabulary. Every Friday we had a vocabulary test, and Sr. B publicly announced each student's test score at the next class. In her high, falsetto-like voice she pronounced good scores to be "super" (or as she pronounced it "SOO-pah"), and she characterized low scores as "punk." So Sr. B's announcing would go something like this: "John Smith—92—supah. Jane Doe—78. Bill Spencer—96—supah. Joe Jones—66—punk. You're in the pit, Boy. Keep it up and you'll flunk the year."

If you never attended Catholic school, you probably think I'm making this all up or at least exaggerating. But I assure you this is really the way Sr. Barbara rolled. If you doubt me, ask any other Catholic school survivor. They know.

The "pit" was Sr. Barbara's subtle metaphor for a punitive/remedial status that required those in it to submit scads of written proof they were studying for the next vocabulary test (in addition to all their other homework). Pit dwellers were thus highly incentivized to climb (claw?) their way out of the academic hole they had dug themselves into. I can imagine the joy they felt upon hearing, "You're out of the pit, Boy." Out of the pit, perhaps, but not yet out of the woods.

When we complained to upperclassmen about Sr. Barbara's harshness they always scoffed at us. "She has really mellowed," they asserted. "You should've had her 3 years ago when she was still tough," they said with pride. Pride to have survived. To have survived the fiery pit, the trial by fire that was Sister Barbara's classroom. We embraced this same proud tone when as seniors we chose for our class motto "Been through hell and still alive, we're the class of '75."

Yes, education was different then than now. It was the last days of a pre-FERPA world, a world in which a short, wiry, bespectacled nun who repeatedly insisted we not call her "Old Poker Face" could publicly praise or shame the performance of her charges. It was a world in which a poker-faced teacher tasked by God to enlighten her students could throw them into a figurative pit and with unquestioned confidence assure them it was for their own good. A world in which nuns believed their students were the ones with the bad habits.

Who ever said nuns don't have a sense of humor?

Breathing the Doctrine Air

Though my parents did their damnedest to make a Catholic out of me, sometime during my teens I misplaced my childhood faith.

When I made my first Confession, my parents presented me with a Catholic Bible. Like *all* Catholic Bibles, it was edged in guilt.

In case you don't know, Confession involves going into a 3-person closet and whispering a list of all your sins to a consecrated man in a black dress. The priest then metes out a penance, often a requirement to say a certain number of "Hail Marys" and "Our Fathers." Once the priest absolves you, your soul is restored to its pristine holy state. In other words, no matter what you've done, if you say a few prayers, you get a clean slate and no longer have to suffer agony in Purgatory. Theologians call this tenet the "Hail Mary Free Pass."

Though some consider this offering of Catholicism to be the deal of a deathtime, it was a deal *breaker* for me. Can you imagine as a 13-year-old having to count up the number of times you had impure thoughts? Is "infinite" a number?

One day at my Catholic high school, Father Cuddy guest-taught our religion class. He put the 15 of us in a big circle and asked what we thought about transubstantiation (the doctrine that during each Mass the priest performs the miracle of transforming bread and wine into the actual body and blood of Jesus). Unanimously, we explained our belief that what the priest did was profoundly symbolic but not really a miracle. We didn't believe that when we took Communion we were literally chewing on Jesus's flesh. After listening to all 15 of us, Fr. Cuddy said matter-offactly, "No, we believe it's the actual body and blood of Christ," and then he moved on to the next topic.

Not only priests but also nuns were instrumental in my Catholic education. Sister Elizabeth, my high school Spanish teacher, for one example, taught me a lot. About three weeks before Christmas when I was a junior, Sr. Elizabeth asked me and Brian Cherer to make a Christmas display on the counter in her classroom. She asked *us* because we were her two best juniors and because the one senior she had first asked hadn't done anything, had dropped the ball. Now it's true that Brian and I dragged our feet, but when we failed to do this non-curricular chore, don't you think the next fair step should have been for Sr. Elizabeth to ask three sophomores? That's not what she did. Instead, she gave me and Brian an early Christmas present—an angry tongue-lashing and a threat that if we didn't quickly deliver, she might lower our grades in the class. Brian and I received this threat like a knee to the groin. Can you really say you've fully lived if you've never been verbally knee-groined by a nun?

Now that Brian and I were properly motivated, we decided to end our nightmare as quickly as possible. That very evening we spent our own money to buy some cheap plastic X-mas "decorations," and we installed them the next day. Sr. Elizabeth taught us how to truly celebrate Christmas: we rushed around in a panic, spent money we hadn't planned to, made a garish religious display, and were relieved when it was all over.

One Catholic sermon I've never forgotten focused on an ecumenical service sponsored by the Catholic Youth Organization (CYO). For five minutes the priest shamed the CYO teens for their poor recruitment since they had succeeded in getting only 12 non-Catholics to attend the special Mass. I have to side with the priest on this one. Where would Christianity be today if Jesus had started out with only a measly 12 disciples?

I went to excellent Catholic schools for eight years. It occurs to me that by supporting good schools, the Catholic church is working at cross purposes with itself. *Cross purposes.* Get it? Ha ha ha.

Catholic schools encouraged us to think, while the entire concept of doctrine required us to *not* think. I'm not Catholic anymore, but, hey, it's their own fault. They educated me too well for me to be comfortable ever again breathing the doctrine air.

Bill Spencer

Love in the Time of Puberty

When I was in the ninth grade, two of my classmates got into a shoving-then-wrestling fight. Surprising because we were in a classroom at the time. In a Catholic high school. Right before Religion class. After one of the school's Sisters of No Mercy broke up the fight, I realized an important insight about my pugnacious peers: they were the victims of puberty.

I've thoroughly researched this topic. "Puberty" comes from the Urbano-American *pubes*, or short, curly, wiry hairs like those that grow above the nether regions of a pubescent boy's upper lip. Soon-to-be sexually armed and dangerous youngsters are flooded with hormones (pronounced "whore moans"). Gonadotropin-releasing hormone (its actual name) cranks boys' testosterone and girls' estrogen factories into overdrive. "Testosterone" sounds like a Mafia movie character to me. Guido Testosterone. (Also known as Mr. T.) Mr. T has a violence code that he promotes to all of his young protégés: "Be a man. Don't take no crap offa nobody." No wonder teen boys feel teste all the time. Girls are another story entirely: between boys and girls there's a vas deferens. For girls, pubescence is a period that begins with the onset of ministration.

I noticed most pubertarian changes when I was thirteen, in eighth grade, when I began to see girls in a thrilling new light. In both boys and girls, chemicals stimulate what Freud termed the "lambada" such that boys and girls become crazed to start making hormonious music together.

Which brings me to our eighth-grade dances. It was the spring of 1971, and the fad in young women's fashion was hot pants. The dances were not school functions, so girls whose blue plaid uniform skirts hid their knees at school

113

were now revealing giddying expanses of naked thigh flesh. Innocent little Angelina Costatexas in a lime-green hot pants suit. Not-quite-so-innocent Sherry Coffee once arrived at a dance, then removed the skirt of her two-piece ensemble to reveal a hot-pants bodysuit. Talk about lambada stimulation! I got to slow-dance with Sherry after her idiot boyfriend broke up with her. She held me so tight I could feel the outline of her aurora borealises. Maybe she was just using me to provoke an ex's jealousy, but my body chemistry didn't even care.

Then there was Amelie Scintilliano. She brought older boys to the dances and spent most of the time on the couch. But she was no couch potato. More like a hot potato. In those days, we thought kissing was "oral sex," but obviously our reasoning was fellatious. Amelie was the most sexually powerful girl in our class, and though I can't confidently comment on her character, for me she had the almost irresistible allure of a bad girl. My own reputation was as a Goody Two-Shoes, a teacher's pet. I was sometimes called "Holy Bill." Which is why at recess one spring day, Amelie Scintilliano angled over my way and began actually talking to me. Amelie wanted to attend an upcoming rock concert scheduled for midday of a weekday in conflict with the school day. She assured me that she had already talked to the school principal, Sister Agitaytus, who said it was OK, that we could leave school for the concert. Later I would realize that I should've inquired about the tone of Sister Agitaytus's voice when she said, "Sure, [if you don't give a damn about your education or your imperiled soul], you can do whatever you want. *Go* to the concert." But at the time, the proximity of Amelie—her svelte but curvy body, the perfume of her long straight dark hair, and the directness of her dark-eyed gaze charmed me, mesmerized me, narcotized my brain. I agreed to go—and that assent began my descent into the downfalls of adulthood. And I don't regret it, not one little bit.

I set out to explain the complex, life-altering maelstrom of puberty and see now that I've mainly just talked about my own sexual fantasies and my easy manipulation at the hands, eyes, and other body parts of women much more confident, more mature, and more powerful than I. I meant to talk about how my class misbehaved so badly that our lay teacher quit before Christmas, how she was replaced by an ex-Marine, how Leonard Velveeta brought a whoopee cushion to class, blew it up, and pretended to cut the cheese, how this elicited a "Sounds like you've got enough gas to get to Poughkeepsie" response from the ex-Marine, and how Lotta Tomboy, a girl whose pituitary couldn't decide which hormones to release, laughed when I sat on a tack that someone—perhaps she—had placed on the seat of my desk.

But, honestly, who can remember such trivia when it's set against the memory of the intoxication of Sherry and the scintillation of Amelie?

Ah, puberty! Good times. Good times.

Human Sexuality 101

I feel so fortunate that I got sexed in college. . . . Sorry, that should read "fortunate that I got Sex Ed in college. . . . Yes, I got lucky.

I took Human Sexuality 101 at Mercer University and chose it for psychology credit. I also could have taken it as a sociology elective. This arrangement is what is known in academia as inter-course credit.

We had a textbook, and there were classroom lectures, but the learning experiences that stand out in my memory the *most* involved the days that our professor brought in anatomically correct, plastic models of the male and female nether regions. That's the scientific term—nether regions. I myself prefer the commoner designation—"crotchal area." On the days these models posed on the professor's desk, the last half hour or so of the classes was devoted to a student-centered lab session. The teacher would appoint a student to be in charge and then leave the room so that students could learn by discovery. This is known as hands-on learning.

The day we were supposed to study the male anatomy model, the teacher chose *me* to lead an exploration into the male reproductive system. Yes, my teacher appointed me head of the penis . . . study group. The blush-provoking details of that session I will not reproduce here.

When it was over, it was *my* job to carry the model across campus to return it to the professor's office. There was a small bag to put the model in—but it was a completely transparent bag. A small study guide slotted into the bag in the exact spot you'd expect to see a fig leaf. A female classmate took pity on me and offered to accompany me as I carried the plastic pelvis—let's call him Elvis—as I carried Elvis through a gauntlet of surprised stares—carried him aloft and proudly.

I do not at all mean to brag about my extensive and deep sexual knowledge when I remind you that the professor chose me as a course leader, nor do I mean to be immodest when I tell you that after I returned Elvis to my professor's secretary and introduced myself, she actually said—this is really true—"So *you're* the brainchild of this class." No, I don't want to brag, so let's just leave it at this, which I know you've been curious about, . . . I got an A.

When Students Grade the Teacher

I'm vain about my teaching ability—so it's not easy for me to admit that my student evaluations over 31 years were less than stellar, were, in fact, quite mixed. As one personnel committee report phrased it, I tended "to sharply polarize student opinion."

My six years of teaching at WCU generated 27 reviews at ratemyprofessors.com, four times the typical number. Many of the evaluations I'll quote from can be verified at this site, including this one: "hard grader, boring speaker, not clear in feedback, expects alot, overall THE DEVIL." This comment is one of my favorites because of the surprise twist at the end. Traditionally, "expects a lot" was considered a *positive* attribute for a teacher, so its placement right before "overall THE DEVIL" caught me off guard. I admire the comic misdirection.

Students' most persistent complaint about me was that my grading standards were too high. "High" is my word. Their words were "harsh," "strict," and "unfair." Consider these 3 assessments:

- "If you want to try hard and make nothing better than a C than this is your professor."
- "If you want to make nothing better than a C on every paper, then take his class."
- "As many of the other reviews have said here, if you want to work yourself to death and make a C, then this class is the one for you."

As these comments indicate, the most common specific student lament was that they were earning only a "C" in my class. Those earning a "D" or an "F" were not the ones complaining. Many, many of my students seemed to regard the "C" grade as cruel and insulting, a punishment, a deliberate, calculated attempt to crush all their aspirations—this despite the fact that my written grading scale described "C" as indicating a satisfactory (though average) performance. Apparently, "average" is a heinous assessment, worse even than "failing/unsatisfactory," perhaps because an "F" would have proved that the professor simply had it in for them.

One of my more creative reviews was "You could turn in your finest work and it will get torn to shreds by this look-alike Hitler." As for the "finest work" reference, why would you turn in anything else in a college-level English class when the professor is widely known as a hard, tough, un-lenient grader? The assumption implied here is that students shouldn't *have* to do their *best* work. As for the "look-alike Hitler" description, I do confess I have a mustache, but I think it makes me look more like Tom Selleck than like Hitler.

My harshest critic wrote, "This guy went out of his way to be a COMPLETE jerk." But I think I've quoted enough reviews already that you know being a jerk wasn't at all "out of my way."

The most constructive criticism I received was this gem: "It is really frustrating to be in his class because I work my ass off and it does not pay off in the end. Also his breath does not smell too good in the morning." The segue from ass-working to bad breath is a little tenuous, but I appreciated the information. A little Colgate, a box of Tic Tacs, and problem solved. I realized I had been eating Cheerios before that class. While I thought my breath was oaty, he obviously thought it was oaty-ous.

If you check me out at ratemyprofessors.com, you'll see that I received no chili peppers for "hotness" and that I scored a 1.8 out of 5 for "easiness" (indicating I was perceived as very hard) and a 3.0 out of 5 for "overall quality." This 3.0 score is symbolized not by a green smiley face or a red frowny face but by a yellow face with a neutral expression. Karma's a bitch: I worked my ass off for my students for over thirty years, and they rated me "average." They gave me the ultimate insult—a "C."

Bill Spencer

That Hussy Edutainment

When I went to college back in the Dim Ages (the 1970s), a mobile device was a bicycle, a text was a book you bought, blackboard was what it sounded like (not an "electronic education platform"), and students wanted an education—a good, solid partner for life. What seems wanted now, however, is edutainment—a metaphorical prostitute, a paid-for good time to be discarded as soon as the moment of pleasure is over.

When I was hired to teach at WCU, I already had 25 years experience teaching college English, so I didn't exactly look forward to the orientation day devoted to improving our teaching skills. Our first session began early in the morning. A veteran history teacher and one of her students huddled at a front corner of the classroom behind the technology-intensive "teacher's station." After we were exhorted to take our teaching from "ordinary to extraordinary," our mentors began blaring Edwin Starr's song "War," then tied men's neckties around their heads and began head-banging their heads in rhythm to the music. As they danced around, I thought, "What is this good for? Absolutely nothing." Our session leader asserted that this would be one way to have an exciting beginning to a class on the history of war. I did admire the performance, but at the same time, I knew I would never expend this much energy or take this big of a risk. If I were willing to make that big of a fool of myself, I would've stayed in university administration. Acting like that in front of a class of sharkish freshmen would be like chunking chum into the water and then jumping in myself.

I'm proud to say that in my thirty-year career I never caved in to students with deficient motivation nor to administrators who constantly pressured me to make

121

learning "fun." My professors had never sung, danced, or otherwise performed for me, and by golly I turned out all right.

Now, I suppose I should confess that in a moment of weakness, for a class on Walt Whitman's poetry, I did once (OK, twenty times) prepare an empty Whitman's Sampler candy box with quotations from Whitman, called these quotations "Whitman samples," and invited each student to pick one and to read it out to the class as a fortune-cookie-like insight into that particular student's nature. Some samples of what they read out to their peers:

—What is commonest, cheapest, nearest, easiest is Me.
—The scent of these armpits aroma finer than prayer.
—Welcome is every organ and attribute of me.
—I am silent, and go bathe and admire myself.
—Do I contradict myself? / Very well then I contradict myself, / (I am large, I contain multitudes.)

It is with shame that I tell you some students laughed and most seemed to enjoy this wicked stunt, this blatant pandering, this regrettable grandstanding.

At least I never stooped to putting on a theatrical performance for my class. Now, I did several times bring a 5-gallon jug into class and act tipsy while a student read the poem "Mr. Flood's Party." Sure I took a few swigs of whiskey-colored apple juice and further acted out the poem's plot by putting the jug down tenderly and croaking out the last words of "Auld Lang Syne," but only when no student would volunteer to take the role. I had to do it then—against my will, you see.

And thank goodness my conscience is clear that I never sang to my students. Well, I don't think singing Emily Dickinson's poem "Because I Could Not Stop for Death" to the tunes of "The Ballad of Jed Clampett" and "The Ballad of Gilligan's Isle" should count. Believe me: my singing cannot be considered entertaining. Besides, I was making an academic point about Protestant hymn meter and its similarity to the ballad stanza. The fact that students may have giggled in no way interfered with the desired pedagogical results.

And I did not in any sense ever dance for my students— not even figuratively. Oh, I may have danced a metaphorical do-si-do with Edutainment a time or two, but I was uncharacteristically intoxicated these times with the vain notion I could be a "popular" teacher. And in our tempestuous tango, I shoved Edutainment away as much as I held her tight, disdained her as often as I dipped her, insulted her as often as I whispered in her ear. And it meant nothing. A meaningless fling.

Yes, I was always faithful to Education. Always. I can truthfully say, "No, I did not have relations with that hussy, Edutainment." I'm not entirely sure what "relations" is, but I know I didn't have any. Ever.

Faculty Senate Fiasco: A Political Primer

Before I ran for Faculty Senate at my university, I was a political naif, a greenhorn, a rube, a babe in the woods, a fish in a barrel, an easy mark, fresh meat, a political joke. You get the picture. Yes, I was a Mr. Smith in a small-scale, low-stakes metaphorical Washington, D.C. And I should have known better. I had heard my father, who once ran and lost a statewide campaign, repeatedly satirize campaign promises by saying, "If I am elected, my troubles will be over, but yours will go on as before."

As soon as I announced my candidacy, a more-knowing colleague asked, "Why would you even want that job?" But I was seduced by the imagined sound of "Senator Spencer." I would get respect, power, and prestige. I would be able to do good. I would think even more highly of myself than ever before. But I didn't get what I expected. What I did get was an education, a doctoral degree if you will, in petty politics. And, believe me, all politics is petty.

After a year of service, I lost my first bid (by humbling self-nomination) to be Vice-President but later won the position in a special election. And I didn't even have to self-nominate the second time because my wife, an alternate Senator filling in, nominated me. I had been in politics only a year and was already exploiting the corrupt benefits of nepotism. Thank you, Sweetheart.

I also learned a lot about a Senator's ability to do good. At my university—hereinafter referred to as FU—as at many universities, the Faculty Senate's actions are not binding. All we could do was make recommendations to university administration, which could then reject our suggestions without even giving a reason. But, first, motions had to win Faculty Senate approval.

The first motion I made as a new Senator was that FU adopt an Honor Code, the result of an hour-long meeting of the Senate's academic subcommittee, which I chaired. I was sure that our lack of an Honor Code was a mere oversight. Who would oppose a code of ethical behavior, a pledge and a reminder to avoid cheating and corruption? But after I made the motion to the full Senate, it was torpedoed by a member of my own subcommittee who had missed our meeting. So I—as well as FU—was still without honor.

A second motion I made was that FU add plus grades as final grade options. I wanted to be able to reward students performing at the higher end of a grade category. When I proposed that this issue be added to the next meeting's agenda, a Senator right behind me said, "That's a bad idea. We have to hand calculate the GPA of all teacher education students." I whipped around in my seat, gave her a "you've-got-to-be-kidding look" and instantly quashed this illogical opposition with a knockout retort: "Don't you have a calculator?" It felt good to so quickly destroy such an absurd objection, and I was proud of my political reflexes—until the next meeting when this same Senator distributed a handout of "10 Reasons to Be Against Plus Grades." "Wow! Ten reasons. That's a lot," I thought. "Ten! I should probably vote against this motion." And, indeed, a majority did vote against it.

My worthy opponent was from the education department, and she had taken me to school, had taught me a lesson in political campaigning. She had taken me to the woodshed. She had beaten me like timpani drums, and I would have to live with the re-percussions. You get the picture. Maybe I should have been more polite to the education Senator, it occurred to me. Maybe I should have been more—what's the word?—politic.

Both of these motions and many others failed to receive even Faculty Senate endorsement. My fellow Senators seemed to think all change was bad. Though I was raised in a Republican household and regarded myself as a conservative, I realized with horror one day that in the context of our Faculty Senate, I wasn't just a liberal; I was a radical. I saw myself as a stately Walter Cronkite while my peers saw me as a shocking Howard Stern. I wasn't Ronald Reagan; I was Ralph Nader. I wasn't Booker T. Washington; I was Malcolm X.

As Senate Vice-President, I was sent to Washington, D.C. to a national Faculty Senates conference entitled "Power and Influence." Here I was told something I already knew—that Faculty Senates have no power or influence—and something I didn't know—that these lacks are by design. Senates are deliberative bodies, constructed to be cautious, slow-moving, and immersed in procedure. What an epiphany! Legislative bodies are *designed* to be frustrating, exhausting time-wasters without power or influence. That way the rate of change is ensured to be a snail's pace, turtle-like, glacial, as slow as molasses, as slow even as the U.S. post office. You get the picture. This way no one gets too uncomfortable or scared.

Actually, it's not entirely true that elected representatives have no power. While they can't put their ideas into effect, they do have the power to kill others' ideas. And there's a particular joy, a delicious schadenfreude in that. This means that in politics those who do not have any ideas are just as powerful as those who do.

So what did I get out of my two years as a politician? I got a firsthand education in political cynicism and an all-expense-paid vacation junket to Washington, D.C. And that ain't bad.

Grocery Store Math

The math "skills" of American students are, by international standards and in technical terms, what is known as "in the toilet"—causing parents and teachers alike to flush.

As reported in the *Washington Post* (Dec. 3, 2013), the Programme for International Student Assessment (PISA) results show that U.S. teens are below average in math skills compared to 64 other countries. The U.S. was outscored by such countries as Latvia, Slovenia, and Vietnam. That's right: in the war of numbers Vietnam has beaten us again. The *San Jose Mercury News* reports that among 34 developed nations, the United States ranked a close-to-the-bottom 26th in math. It's an acute problem, a sine of the times.

It's customary after such negative numbers become public to decry the U.S. educational system, the political system, and the degradation of the family unit, but on a recent jaunt to secure some Spicy Sweet Chili Doritos, I had an epiphany as to the true cause our students are confused about numbers—and not just even numbers, even odd numbers. Squarely at the root of the math problem in America—is the grocery store.

Sauntering down the paper goods aisle, I noticed several bathroom tissue packages with large equations printed on them. For example, a pack of a dozen rolls of Scott tissue brazenly asserted for every passerby to see that 12 = 36. I remember from my own school daze that the two parallel lines in an equation mean "equals." So I'm quite surprised that the Scott company would claim that 12 is equal to a number that I was taught is 4 times as much as 12. But then I saw that Angel Soft bathroom tissue backed Scott's dubious math with their own allegation that 12 = 36. I was even more confused when I spied a different pack of 12 Angel Soft rolls that advertised 12 = 26. So according to Angel Soft, 12 = 26 <u>and</u> 12 = 36, a difference of almost 10. Cottonelle teaches us that 12 = 24, while Charmin instructs that 12 = 24 <u>and</u> 12 = 48. Charmin's theorem that 24 = 48 is confirmed by both Cottonelle and Quilted Northern except that Quilted Northern subverts its own math by also proposing 24 = 54. Angel Soft boldly goes it alone with their equation 24 = 58. Sometimes the equations get all fuzzy as when Charmin posits that 12 is "more than 24," which in equation form could look like 12 > 24 or 12 = 24+. What all this adds up to is bathroom tissues are just as soft on math as they are on our backsides. Clearly toilet paper is tearing at the very tissue of our society; it's shredding our children's sagging math skills. No wonder we're near the bottom.

Additionally, paper towels also figure into our children's declining math abilities. Bounty educates us that 12 = 16, 12 = 18, and 12 = 20, plus that 6 = 8 and 2 = 5. Brawny tries to convince us that 3 = 4, 6 = 9, and 8 = 14 while Sparkle postulates that 8 = 12 and 6 = 10. Among paper towels only Decorator goes into the advanced math of fractions with their equation 3 = 3½. Though my second-grade teacher, Mrs. Carter, would not have assented to Decorator's arithmetic, she would have agreed that of all the publicized paper-goods equations 3 = 3½ comes the closest to being accurate. Among paper-goods companies, Decorator is a math genius.

The common denominator in what I've exposed so far is the mind-blowing equations trumpeted by paper goods, but when you look for other culpable products, you'll find that soda pops. Yes, diet Mtn Dew seems equally bent on multiplying our students' woes. The 7.5-ounce can of diet Mtn Dew indicates in writing that it contains 0 calories. The 12-ounce can/bottle also reports that it contains 0 calories. So how many calories are in a 16-ounce bottle of diet Mtn Dew? Take a moment to carefully calculate your answer. OK. I'm sure you arrived at the correct response of 5 calories. That's what the bottle says. You can check it yourself. So if there are 5 calories in 16 ounces, how many calories are there in a 2-liter bottle? You'll be relieved to learn from the label that the 2-liter bottle contains "0 calories per 12 ounces." If you're at all like me, you realize that diet Mtn Dew math tells us something very important: avoid the 16-ounce bottle at all costs. Who needs the calories?

In sum, I can count on one hand the dozens of reasons our students are lagging behind students in other countries in math. All of these equilibrium-disturbing equations are a prime example of how grocery stores are a factor in ruining the fundamentals of math understanding in this country. Our students' math test scores are simply a product of product advertising. If you can't count on the ad divisions of American corporations, whom can you count on? I believe there's a conspiracy to create mathematical chaos in this country. I call this my chaos theory. In equation form it looks like this: Grocery Store Equations – Mathematical Chaos. American grocery stores are derailing math education, getting our students off track, one train having left Bentonville, Arkansas at 7:00 a.m. traveling east at 60 mph. When product after product indiscretely blazons that $12 = 24 = 48 = 56$, the problem is as easy to figure as $2 + 2 = \ldots$ Oh, who knows what the hell $2 + 2$ equals anymore? But I do know that if I had 2 apples and a grocery store gave me 1.14 more apples what I'd have. . . . I'd have pie. I'd eat half of it myself and share the other 65% with you.

Cormac McCarthy Catharsis

Before Cormac McCarthy won a National Book Award or a Pulitzer Prize, before *No Country for Old Men* won an Oscar, and before *The Counselor* was panned as the worst movie of the year with the worst scene of the year—back when most of McCarthy's novels were out of print and he was known as a writer's writer (i.e. he hadn't sold many books)—I chose him as the subject of my dissertation.

At this point I'd like to tell you that the reason I was drawn to McCarthy is that his novels foreground a Morpheus-ological Trinity, a Neo-Matrix in a Deconstructionist critical approach. I'd *like* to tell you that, but it's just not true. The truth is that I thought McCarthy's novel *Suttree* was one of the funniest books I'd ever read. And one of the best. That novel—about a lapsed Catholic on a spiritual quest—grabs me and speaks to me like no other.

I now realize that choosing a dissertation topic is like choosing a friend, someone you're going to spend a lot of good and bad times with and who's going to help you learn about yourself. My "friendship" with McCarthy has been a hoot, and one thing I've learned is that our shared Catholic upbringings led to a need to overcome a lot of repression.

By the time I'd read McCarthy's first five novels, I knew how he'd earned the label "Southern Grotesque." There's a scene in *Suttree* when the title character engages with his prostitute companion in a game of "vying to elaborate the most outrageous perversions." And McCarthy himself seems to have played that game as part of his writing process. His novels include voyeurs, pedophiles, brother-sister incest, father-daughter incest, "silkbedizen pizzlelickers," and a character we might call a "fruitophile" or accuse of "fruitiality," sometimes referred to as the "moonlight melonmounter."

In *Child of God*, McCarthy's protagonist, Lester Ballard, is a cross-dressing necrophile. A whole novel about a necrophile. I was once invited to guest lecture on Lester Ballard for a Southern Studies class at Ole Miss and was told parking legally on campus would be challenging, but my host (Tom Rankin) said if I got a ticket, he'd fix it. When I did indeed receive a citation and notified Tom, he said, "Don't worry. I'll take care of it. I'll just tell the police that you were on campus to talk about a guy who has sex with dead people."

By the time I began writing my dissertation, I was ready to follow McCarthy's own lead in the sense-of-humor department and see how many bawdy puns I could get away with. And I did sneak some in, including my tome's title "The Extremities of Cormac McCarthy." I was feeling less repressed already.

After I finished a draft, I remember that a big moment for mc was Spell Checking the document. This was before AutoCorrect. My computer was a primitive IBM that needed five 5¼" floppy disks to boot it up. There was no mouse, only F keys, and back in those days Spell Check programs had glossaries that were incomplete and, as it turns out, prudish. With my wife, who had word-processed the entire document, present and her computer-expert nephew at the keyboard, we began the orthographical search of my two-year-long doctoral study with an air of formal ceremony. We watched intently as the search stopped on the following words, each highlighted in yellow: "Shit," "goddamned," "shit," "goddamned," "shit," "shat," "shit," "shit," "shit," "drunkern shit," "goddamned," "goddamn broncpeeler," "Fuck," "shit-for-brains," "chickenshit," "goddamn," "cacodemons," "othersuttree," "cunt," "cunt," and "donkeyengine." It was a veritable parade of profanity taken from quotations of the novels.

The third time "shit" was highlighted, my wife's nephew looked up. At the seventh occurrence, he asked incredulously, "This is your dissertation?" McCarthy was a friend, all right—like those friends from childhood that your parents regarded as too-knowing bad influences.

By this point, McCarthy had helped me make real progress in wriggling out of my Catholicism straitjacket, but there was a final maneuver to master—reading my scholarship in public. I should tell you that during all of my scholastic career I was regarded by teachers as a well-behaved model student, mocked by peers in the eighth grade as "Holy Bill." Similarly, as an English professor I was respected as serious and even-keeled. So colleagues were surprised when at a conference at my own university, I read an essay entitled "The Excremental Vision of Cormac McCarthy." I hope you can imagine the guilty fun I had searching out every one of the many scatological references in McCarthy's body of work. And the delight I took in sharing my findings with a packed audience expecting the usual scholarly presentation. I argued that McCarthy attacked human pretensions and pride in the satirical tradition of Swift and Rabelais and offered evidence that included the following:

> In addition to the scores of times the word "Shit" is used as an expletive in *Suttree*, there are also many references to animal turds and two humbling references to found "human stool." Suttree remembers the story about how his Uncle Milo drowned when he went down with a "bargeload of birdshit." The ghetto-like area of Knoxville where Suttree lives is known as McAnally Flats, a name that has the word "anal" embedded in it. The ragman refers to all of life as "that crapgame." His reference implies an

existential emphasis on chance but also
further suggests that "crap" is somehow the
essence of life. Finally, in *Suttree* even the
sun is considered as perhaps just "a
bunghole to a greater hell beyond."

I met McCarthy once. I expected him to be taller. But his deep voice did not disappoint. A voice for speaking forbidden words. A voice for violating taboos.

After I presented my papers in public, my exorcism was complete. I was a free man. And I owe it all to you, Cormac. Thank you. You've been one hell of a good friend.

This & That

The Evolution of Cool

When I saw a list of popular musicians and bands recently, I thought I might be a victim of slightly early onset dementia. I could make almost no sense of it:

Trae Tha Truth ft. Diddy, Jeezy, & T.I.
A$AP Mob ft. A$AP Nast & Method Man
Big Boi ft. Big K.R.I.T. & UGK & Blue Oyster Cult.

"Is any of this English?" I thought. Is it some kind of code? The name that disoriented me the least because it's been around the longest is actually the most surrealistic and nonsensical—Blue Oyster Cult. A cult devoted to blue oysters? It dawned on me that my own sense of "cool" has become outdated. My own sensibilities stopped progressing at some point while the popular concept of cool continued to change. I'm fossilizing. I'm unable to fully appreciate the alluring cachet of names like Charli XCX, 2 Chainz, Skooly, ScHoolboy Q, Juicy J, Pimp C, and Will. I. Am.

I haven't always been so out of touch with cool. And I do know enough to look for it among band names rather than, say, names of law firms. Yes, popular music has always reflected the contemporaneous idea of what's "with it" and "now." No matter how rich or corporate they might actually be, musicians have rarely been associated with "The Man." No, instead they are seen as among those who *stick it* to The Man. I've come to realize that cool is an attitude madly admired by the very young and loathed by the very old. By this gauge, I'm old but not yet "very old." I don't loathe current band names; they just confuse me.

In the 1960s I recognized the requisite anti-establishment rebellion inherent in such names as The Beatles. It was often an orthographical deviation, a one-letter misspelling as also found in Monkees, Byrds, Led Zeppelin, and Creedence. Just that one-letter difference let us know that these bands were too cool for school rules. No matter how much society had spent on their education, they'd spell their names however the hell they wanted to. These bands were courageously nonconformist. Yeah, they were far-out, man. Additionally, many 60s bands were attuned to the power of the definite article "The": The Beatles, The Rolling Stones, The Beach Boys, The Who, The Doors, The Kinks, The Temptations, The Moody Blues. These weren't just *some* rolling stones; they were *The* Rolling Stones. And they weren't just *any* who. Sixties bands realized the uniqueness and ultimateness bestowed by this unassuming three-letter powerhouse in such designations as the Pope or the President. If someone called you up and said, "This is Stephen King," a natural response would be to ask, "*The* Stephen King?" These *The* bands were the bomb.

A new development among 1970s band names was the belief that suave nonchalance could be implied simply by exploiting a typographical symbol—the ampersand. Why be hyper-correct and overly lettery with "and" when "&" does the same trick with much more sprezzatura? This was the aesthetic emulated by Kool & the Gang; Sly & the Family Stone; Crosby, Stills, Nash & Young; and Earth, Wind, & Fire. (Earth, Wind, & Fire originally also auditioned Water but rejected it since it ruined the rockin' flow of monosyllables.) These ampersand bands were awesome.

In the 1980s . . . Oh, who are we kidding? Cool took a holiday during the 80s.

Band names of the 1990s compose a weird restaurant menu of spices, delicacies, and dainties: Red Hot Chili Peppers, The Cranberries, The Smashing Pumpkins, Hootie & the Blowfish, Pearl Jam, Ice Cube—and, for dessert, a single Eminem, your choice of plain or peanut. Among nineties band names, food was hot.

In the 1990s and in the new millennium, cool apparently suffered from a much shorter shelf life as indicated by individual performers changing their self-chosen freaky deaky names—once, twice, or even more times. Name changes showed a commitment to keeping it fresh. Calvin Broadus traded Snoop Doggy Dogg for Snoop Dogg, then Snoop Lion, then Snoopzilla. Sean Combs tweaked his musical moniker to Puff Daddy, then P. Diddy, then just plain Diddy or sometimes Swag. Prince Rogers Nelson—Prince—pushed the envelope till it burst by exchanging his name for an invented unpronounceable symbol that looked something like a male symbol stick figure crossed by a stylized trumpet, a trumpet presumably blaring out, "The Artist Formerly Known as Prince." Stick figure or not, it didn't stick. This symbol, which Prince insisted meant Love Symbol No. 2, was so cool it was frosty, which is the kind of reception it got.

Yes, the evolution of band names is a history of the ever-changing concept of cool—from Kajagoogoo to Lady Gaga; from Kool & the Gang to LL Cool J to Coolio; from U2 to UB40 to E-40; from the King to the Boss to the Prince of Pop. It's a chronicle of artistic rebellion, a timeline of the search for a name that says, "We are totally unique—exactly like all of you." It's a record of the quest for a name that signals, "We just like playing music; we don't give a damn about money" but which also promotes making millions and millions of dollars.

And what could be cooler than cool millions? That kind of cool never does change.

Meeting, the Enemy

Meetings are the cold, muck-filled trenches in which turf wars are fought. They are the Texas Death Matches of the business world. They are corporate roller derbies. People just trying to skate by spin their wheels, go in circles, and end up exactly where they began—but only after a lot of elbowing, back shoving, and punching. Can you think of any other supposedly civil event that has necessitated an entire book of procedural protocol to keep people from choking each other?

Although there are different types of meetings, *all* are futile depleters of time and energy. (In meetings even the *minutes* take hours.)

First, there's the perilous "Rubber Stamp" meeting, when all those present are obliged to approve, in fact *commend*, some foregone decision. However, the actual nature of the session is never announced, so unwary new recruits may stick their heads up out of the "No Man's Land" trench to blithely offer "suggested improvements." The machine gun of disfavor quickly converts them into cautious veterans— if it doesn't kill them, of course.

Then, there's the popular "Geyser" meeting, when participants are encouraged to impotently vent their complaints until they've completely run out of steam. They are conditioned to view this gas-passing as "having a voice" and as "entering the conversation." As a morale management technique, this one's an Old Faithful.

Finally, there's the "Mob Mentality" meeting (which feels like a prison sentence), justified by the view that fifteen heads are better than one. (Have you noticed that every mob is an *angry* mob?) The doctrine here is that problem-solving is best accomplished by large groups of people forced to sit in a cramped cell while they are uncomfortable, bored, and fearful of reprisals from the warden or from other inmates. Contrary to doctrine, however, meetings actually incentivize the meeters to suppress thinking and to agree to whatever is *first* proposed, no matter how stupid. Opposition or questioning leads to chaotic bickering, which prolongs the ordeal. "We're tacking thirty minutes onto your sentence for resisting and obstruction." Going along constitutes "good behavior" and is the quickest way to secure your release.

But even if meeters were reckless enough to disregard the threat to their job security and to disregard the danger of destroying the fragile, hard-won cease-fire among contentious co-workers, and would boldly say what they really thought—even *then* meetings wouldn't work to produce the best thinking.

Did *Origin of Species* originate while Darwin slouched at a table with a pack of not-very-evolved colleagues? No, that link is missing.

Did Shakespeare write his plays during a Globe-al teleconference? Methinks not.

Did Jules Verne invent the Nautilus in *sub*-committee? Naut-a-chance!

Sir Isaac Newton was completely alone, *not* in a compulsory gathering of fellow physicists, when he devised the law now known as Robert's *Third* Rule of Order—that for every motion there is an equal and opposite counter-motion such that no progress shall ever be made. Newton also formulated a *First* Rule of Order, but, tragically, his entire theory of motion "died for lack of a second."

Finally, in meeting after meeting during the 1860s Russian chemist Dmitri Mendeleev made the motion that rows and columns be used to arrange the chemical elements into a chart, but his idea was periodically tabled. That's just sad.

It's time to call the question. Why do we still have meetings? Trench warfare has been abandoned as outdated.

Nobody watches roller derby anymore. And indentured servitude has been abolished. So why can't we rid ourselves of these grueling time wasters? Do we need a constitutional amendment? Let's form an ad hoc committee. We'll meet 5:00 Friday afternoon in Meeting Room B.

Jury Doody

If you have a choice between shoveling horse manure and serving on a jury, go with the manure mucking every time, nolo contendere. The two jobs pay about the same, and being a juror involves more stalling and more waste; it's by far the tougher duty. At least with manure disposal, you can see you've improved matters and done the right thing. I feel compelled, pro bono, to raise a sustained objection to the "criminal" treatment of juries, and I hereby summon you to judge for yourself the merits of my case.

Jury duty under our current system of juris-imprudence is like being under the scrutiny of TSA agents for a week. You can be incarcerated just for joking around. So a "humorist" is persona non grata. As a juror you're basically under arrest until the judge pardons you. You don't eat, sleep, or go home unless the judge says so. Nor, though a jury is ipso facto "peers," are you allowed willy nilly to go to the bathroom.

"Objection, Your Honor. The lame vulgar pun on "peers" clearly constitutes "joking around.""

"Sustained. Strike that last sentence from the record, and all of you are hereby ordered to disregard it."

I've served on two juries, and both times had splitting headaches but no access to pain relief. On my first jury I was told I couldn't take notes. Then during deliberation, when we asked for a trial transcript so we could review the testimony, we were told no. On TV, juries always get a transcript and videotapes and whatever else they ask for. But real-life jurying is nothing like TV.

On TV, trials are always high-stakes, suspenseful murder cases with surprising revelations. The second jury I "sat on," gluteus maximus, heard, ad infinitum, the case of a defendant who had been previously convicted of shoplifting a single pair of socks, valued, I'm guessing, at no more than $2. The case was an appeal, but not an appealing case. That's right—two trials for one pair of socks. The defendant had picked up a pack of three pair of socks connected by a monofilament, then had bitten through the monofilament and put on one pair of the socks in the store before paying. His savvy lawyer argued that his client was not an intentional shoplifter, only an idiot.

Once we jurors were in the jury room, one woman immediately began expressing her fear of reprisals from the defendant if we voted to uphold his conviction. He didn't strike me as much of a threat, but clearly this woman was very afraid. Sigourney Weaver in *Alien* didn't act any more terrified. In the first two votes, she cast the lone "not guilty" vote. She explained, "I don't want him coming after me." For an hour we worked to calm her and encourage her, and on the third written vote, though still saying how scared she was, she made the "guilty" verdict unanimous.

After we returned to the courtroom and delivered our verdict, the judge thanked us for our service and, to my great relief, dismissed us. Half of us were literally out the door when the defendant's attorney asked to poll the jury. He asked us to verbally state our verdict vote, which went smoothly until he asked Sigourney and she went all non compos mentis on us and said, "I'm not sure." Our hearts sank, and the judge ordered us back to the jury room. We had been un-dismissed.

After the judge learned our vote had been written, he instructed us to dig through the trash to recover the slips of paper and then to pick out our vote based on the handwriting. Back in the courtroom, we were each asked, "Is this the vote you wrote down?" and when we all answered "yes," we were once again dismissed and this time sprinted for the door.

I've often wondered if our vicious sock thief ever did in fact pursue a vendetta against the terrified member of our posse comitatus. Come to think of it, I'm not sure he hasn't been targeting me for retribution. Over the years I've been unable to account for several pairs of allegedly "lost" socks.

Nota bene: what matters most on a jury is not what you don't do; what matters most is what you do do. And if the evidence is incomplete, do not be deterred. Consider the facts carefully and anal-yze them. Go with your gut. I hope you never receive a jury summons, but if you do, then know what to expect. Take a shovel—because if you're on a jury, my friend, then I'm afraid you're going to be up to your neck in some serious, deep duty.

Outhouse Racing Right up My Alley

When I found out that only 25 miles from my home there'd be outhouse races—outdoor potty houses on skis competitively sliding down a snowy slope—I couldn't wait to "go."

As soon as I arrived at Ski Sapphire Valley, I checked out the lineup of contestant vehicles, most of them made from wood and all of them fulfilling the requirements of a "seat with at least one hole" and "a roll of toilet paper or alternative wiping source."

The names of the entries really appealed to my Rabelaisian sense of humor: One of my favorites was a Flintstones-themed racer called Yabba Dabba Doo-Doo. Another favorite, Poop Coop, was constructed mainly of chicken wire and feathers and was later piloted by a man-sized yellow chicken.

The Humane Society-sponsored K-9 Urination Station looked like a giant red fire hydrant. At race time, a giant dog occupied the "driver's" seat. I'm pretty sure this entry is the reason the event was scheduled to be live-streamed.

Other entries included Party Pooper, Taking Care of Business, Royal Flush, and Who Cut the Cheese? Sometimes, people really restore your faith in humanity.

Each entry had a three-person team: two pushers and one to sit inside the contraption as it hurtled down the slope unsteerable and without brakes. I don't think these riders have an official title, but I'd suggest "privy pilots," "commode commanders," or perhaps "john jockeys." These people are intrepid, possessing absolutely no end of derring-doo.

The racers compete two at a time, and it's a double "elimination" contest, so each team gets to go at least twice. The heats are known as "runs," and, believe me, there's nothing like a whole afternoon of runs. Teams have to push their privies up the slope themselves, so there's a good bit of effort and straining involved before anything happens.

The race begins by pitting #1 against #2. Savvy readers have by now realized that, really, the whole thing is a contest focused on #1 and #2.

The outhouse sleds often bump into each other or veer off center and hit the snow bank lining the course, so there are some hair-raising crashes, better known in outhouse racing circles as "accidents" or "wipeouts." I'm not sure which term is more appropriate. Which sounds better: "Several people in outhouses had accidents," or "several people seated in outhouses ended up wiping out?" These falling-over failures are so common that even finishing the run is basically a crap shoot. When the inside riders survive these spills unharmed, I can assure you everybody is relieved.

Often it's hard to tell who's winning since *every* entry is always a head. But on this day it came down to a final run between Poop Coop and Confession Session, an outhouse in the guise of a little white church with angel wings painted on the sides. Poop Coop flew down the slope. It was beautiful, like watching poultry in motion. But apparently angels fly even faster than fowl, for on this fine day, it was ultimately Confession Session that would sit upon the throne. Did it win because it was the hole-iest? Who can say?

If you're a student of scatology, outhouse racing may be right up your alley, too. How often do you get to see someone dressed as a poo emoji do a victory dance? How often do you get to attend an event that all day long it's just one big potty atmosphere?

Was it totally perfect? Maybe not. But I do think it truthfully can be said that in the end, everything came out all right.

Any Pet in a Storm

When my stepson's cat, Pishi (Farsi for "Kitty," pronounced PEE-shee), came to live with us for a year, she didn't warm to me right away. Early on, when I tried to pet her, she bit me, and it wasn't a love bite. Later, after seeing Pishi blitz out the door to attack a dog five times her size, I realized I'd gotten off easy. I love cats and continued to court Pishi's favor, but our relationship stayed strained. Until the ice storm.

The ice storm of 1994 gifted us in the Mississippi Delta with a tree-destroying, power-pole-snapping eight inches of ice. Eight. We thought the first evening without electricity was fun, romantic even, as we played the game of Life by candlelight. But that was before we heard we'd be without power for weeks perhaps. Our only heat source was a small wood-burning fireplace in the living room, so we dragged a mattress right to the edge of the hearth.

A stray, Pishi had been taken in by my wife and her former husband years earlier in Knoxville, coincidentally during a winter storm. Pishi was a survivor and could tell my wife was a soft touch. She had laid siege to my wife's heart with her bedraggled fur and kitty-cat eyes and camped out on the doorstep until the door was opened.

During our Delta ice storm, Pishi's survival instinct kicked into high gear again. Paramount to her was warmth. She got as close as she could to the fire, pushing against the center of the fireplace screen so hard that we feared she'd singe her fur. She was a fireplace hog, and whenever we tried to move her, she hissed at us.

Before the ice storm, I hadn't realized how human Pishi was. One night after we'd gone to bed, I heard a noise in the kitchen and discovered Pishi on top of the kitchen table eating glazed doughnuts. The next night, there she was again, this time eating spicy Doritos from a bag. I fully expected to find her the third night sipping cognac and smoking a cigar.

But her strange appetite wasn't even what was most surprising. The first night that we slept on the mattress by the fire, a very odd thing happened. After we got under the covers, Pishi came to my side of the bed, her head only inches from mine, and stared at the covers right where they were pulled up to my neck—as if she wanted in. But that couldn't be right; she always slept with my stepson. She was *his* cat. She stared so long that finally I picked her up and took her to my stepson's side of the mattress. My stepson lifted the blanket for her, but she demurred and catwalked back over to me and resumed her previous insistent stance and icy stare. Eventually, I relented, and she spent the night curled against my chest. I may not have been her favorite person, but she chose me as her bed partner for the entire week. Apparently, she decided proximity to me gave her the best chance of living through the cold.

My wife might share Pishi's belief. When she tells me I have a hot body, I know she doesn't mean it's sexy; she means I literally radiate a high body temperature. Many nights when she complains how cold she is, I wake drenched in sweat and throw off layers of blankets. In the summer, she keeps her distance and complains, "You're a furnace." But when winter comes, my hotness is a real asset. Then, my wife, Pishi-like, snuggles up close.

Pishi and I bonded during that icy crisis, and I've come to see parallels between that relationship and others. My advice to those trying to find a place in an already-existing family structure is to capitalize on your assets and to exploit the circumstances. Me? I used my hot body. And thanked God for an ice storm.

Who's the Silly Goose Now?

I used to live near a city park pond where several domestic geese resided. A wide paved walking path skirted the back of the pond, and at any season other than early spring, my wife, Carolyn, and I took this path as part of our soothing daily walks in the park. We avoided the pond path in the spring unless the geese were swimming or on the opposite side because we knew they could be aggressive if there were eggs or hatchlings around.

One spring day we checked and saw that the geese were lazily floating at the farthest-away corner and felt lucky and grateful that our favorite route wasn't closed to us. When we were about a third of the way down this path, however, we noticed that all six or seven geese suddenly started swimming toward us. I'd never seen this behavior before. "Have you ever seen 'em do that, Carolyn?" No, she hadn't either. They were so far away they couldn't possibly be upset at us. Nevertheless, Carolyn and I changed our pace from stroll to fast hike. But when we sped up, so did the geese. They were straining their necks now, and they were on a direct collision course.

Now there's a funny thing about my relationship to wild animals that occurred to me then. I basically depend on wild animals being afraid of me and either ignoring me or running away when they see me. But here was a flotilla of apparently angry geese bearing down on me at attack speed with what I realized was the intention to do me some bodily harm. And not just me but also my wife. While my self-preservation instinct was revving up, I was also acutely conscious of my manly role as protector of the womenfolk. I also realized the absurdity—the comicalness—of my circumstances. I remembered the unrelenting mockery President Jimmy Carter was subjected to when a swimming vicious rabbit attacked his canoe. And I remembered a story Carolyn had told me about one of her cousins—a guard at a corporate facility that included a pond. One time when she was patrolling the pond perimeter, a goose sneaked up behind her and bit her on the butt. She didn't know what was happening and instinctively drew her pistol. Company policy required guards to file a report whenever they pulled their weapons, so she was soon a laughingstock, constantly being asked, "Have you had any more gunfights with pissed-off poultry?" and "*Where* did it bite you again?"

So bearing all this in mind—the physical threat to both me and my wife, my role as manly protector, and the risk of embarrassment and ridicule—I swiftly decided on a course of action and took control of the situation. I turned to Carolyn and said, "Run!"

Maybe that sounds like a less-than-brilliant plan to you, but it was in fact a solid solution. We could run (properly motivated) faster than the attack geese could swim, so we might have to sacrifice our dignity, but we were going to escape the threatened confrontation.

Except for one little flaw in the plan. When we began to run, the geese started flapping their wings and in two seconds were airborne.

To this day, *The Wizard of Oz* is one of the scariest movies I've ever seen. It terrified me as a child, and in the whole movie, the most frightening scene to me is the flying monkeys.

That's how I felt as the geese flew straight at us. When they reached us, they streaked at eye level only two feet from our heads, exactly matching our speed and paralleling our course. They were so close we heard their wing flap. Chased by flying monkeys. My nightmare come true. I had no brain, no heart, no courage. I certainly had no dignity.

And as I fled for my life in unabashed terror, I wondered why I had even *come* on this walk. Why did I ever leave the house when after all—"there's no place like home; there's *no* place . . . like home."

Bill Spencer

Scared Dumb

"Sorry, Venkman, I'm terrified beyond the capacity for rational thought." —Egon in *Ghostbusters*

Once in my life, and once only, I was scared speechless—*literally* speechless. I wanted to speak, but terror had erected a blazing barricade on the road between my brain and vocal cords. Of all my reactions to fear over the years, this was the dumbest.

What occasioned this unspeakable horror? A small child, probably 8 or 9 years old. And what did she do to trigger my wordless panic? She opened the door to her house.

Now, before you start questioning my testicular fortitude, let me explain the series of events that, for a 10-second eternity, rendered me completely mute.

I was 14, delivering newspapers on my bike route, when I decided it was also a good time to canvass for new *Daily Sun* subscribers. As I stopped at one house, I noticed a solid-black cat in the driveway. Although I didn't consider myself superstitious, I'd seen my father more than once hang a U-turn if a black cat crossed the road in front of him. This witch's familiar crossed the street and slinked up the driveway of the house that I wanted to solicit as a new subscriber, so I ended up following it. The drive led into a double carport with two steps up to a side door into the house, which is the one I decided to knock on. As I entered the carport, I noticed it was dimly lit with an eerie green light. This seemed strange, so I looked up and saw that there was a skylight, where a rectangle of the solid roof had been replaced with corrugated semi-opaque green plastic. As I went to the door, the black cat followed.

At the door, I could hear some music playing inside the house, and it didn't take long for me to recognize it as the strident, spooky theme music to a TV show, a popular Vampire soap opera called *Dark Shadows*.

So to recap what was stewing in my unconscious—a black cat had acquired me and led me across the street to a weirdly greenish-lit carport attached to a house with Vampire music playing inside. As I said, I'm not very superstitious, but the bizarre confluence of these unnerving elements was starting to get to me. Maybe I didn't really *need* any more subscribers.

The truth is, whenever you go up to a strange house and knock on the door, you have no idea who or what is going to answer. The door is going to open on the unknown, and what could be more frightening than that?

Before I describe the little girl, let me point out that things that ordinarily seem harmless can sometimes *become* horrifying. Is Chucky just a little doll? Is Pennywise just a clown? Is the flaming Stay-Puft Marshmallow Man just a big toasted confection?

So the door atop the steps slowly opens. I don't remember any creaking. And there above me stood the little girl.

Reflexively, my head snapped down and to the left to avoid her gaze—to avoid being turned to stone, I suppose—while my heart began auditioning for the cannon volley part in the "1812 Overture."

She was short, with unusually pale skin and unnaturally yellow, dead-straight hair. But I think it was her eyes that had made me most react. They were larger and rounder than ordinary, with the brightest white sclera I think I've ever seen—except for the visible red capillaries zigzagging across the eyeballs. They were Bride-of-Frankenstein eyes. At least that's the way my brain interpreted the nanosecond's worth of information my eyes had taken in before I had turned away. Another way of saying it would be that she was a petite, bright-eyed blond girl—but I stood my ground. Because cowards don't run in my family.

She politely asked, "Can I help you?" and although I wanted to respond, my brain was on lockdown. The inmates were rioting, but they couldn't get out. I thought, "I hope this isn't permanent. I hope this is only aphasia I'm going through." Finally, I was able to blurt out, "Would you like to subscribe to the *Daily Sun*?" She said she'd ask her mother.

While she was gone, with Vampire voices in the background, I started a mental mantra: "*Please* don't subscribe to the paper. *Please* don't subscribe," and when she returned, she quietly said, "No thank you." The child of *Dark Shadows* would be letting no *Daily Sun* into her life, after all.

I was saved. Saved!

And I set a new bicycle speed record pedaling to the next house—almost flying—like the first bat out of hell.

Mississippi Skeeters

Mosquitoes in the Mississippi Delta, where I lived for 25 years, were so bad that you're not going to believe me when I tell you.

They were so bad that when they covered the two walls and ceiling of our carport every summer, we could actually hear the eerie hum.

They were so bad that we once thought a friend's baby had the measles when actually he was just covered in mosquito-bite welts.

They were so bad that our town had not only a fleet of malathion-fogger trucks but also its own mosquito air force for dropping larvicide over the ditches, bogues, and bayous.

So bad that when a relative from New Orleans visited, he said,"You can't scare me 'cause I live in a city that's below sea level," but after he'd spent 15 minutes swatting and scratching while driving us around at night, he said, "You're right. This is unbelievable."

So bad that I gave up trying to kill them with flying insect spray or yard fogger because that just riled them up and made them swarm. Seriously.

So bad that I constantly tried new methods to keep them away from our front door. I rigged up two metered sprayers on either side of the door and saturated the door itself with Deep Woods Off. I burned citronella candles and torches and mosquito coils—and I tried electric fans both inside and outside the door and once tried putting a heater outside the door to make the Delta's sweltering summer sauna even more prohibitively searing for the little suckers.

Whenever my wife, stepson, and I planned to enter or exit the house, we'd gather in a tight pack; I'd ask, Ready?" then violently throw open the door; and we'd all spring together over the threshold and slam the door behind us.

Even with all this, every time we opened the front door, two or three or five or six mosquitoes dive-bombed through the breach.

There were two schools of thought in the Delta about what to do once mosquitoes got into your house. One philosophy was that nothing could be done, that it was an obnoxious but irremediable fact of life that simply had to be accepted—like Republicans. One such disciple in this faith was the aforementioned friend with the measle-y baby.

But in our household this thinking was heresy; we didn't believe in mosquito-bite martyrdom. We kept two flyswatters and a can of flying insect killer just inside the front door. After we leaped in and slammed the door, we'd each grab a weapon and scan the walls. We all got pretty good at grabbing mosquitoes out of the air with one-handed squeezes or two-handed claps, but smashing them against the wall was a higher-percentage kill. Often after a wall kill, particularly a bloody one, I'd laugh in a theatrical way and then growl, "Leave it . . . as a warnin' to the others."

I told you you wouldn't believe me.

We competed for most kills, and no claim counted unless a visible dead body could be produced. We did not rest. We constantly studied the walls for dark specks, and we routinely ambushed the tiny devils in the showers, one of their favorite spots. We knew their crazed flight patterns, and once we spotted one, we dropped whatever we were doing and hunted it down and killed it. If we were in the middle of a meal or a conversation, that didn't matter. Sometimes when guests saw us jump up and begin snatching at the air, they would look on open-mouthed—in awe, I'm sure, of our highly honed skill.

Because of these quite-normal, not-at-all-obsessive actions, by bedtime each night we usually had a bloodsucker-free home. But sometimes we didn't. In the middle of the night, I'd hear a buzzing right in my ear or would wake to a fresh, itchy bite. Others might have pulled up the covers more and tried to go back to sleep, but that's not what we did in our house. Instead, I'd announce, "Mosquito!" as I jumped out of bed to turn on the light. Then my wife and I would sit up in bed with our backs tightly against the wall to prevent backbites, and we'd wait. We'd wait as long as it took. We'd wait until that pesky little sleep spoiler was a scarlet inkblot on somebody's hand. That's when we'd go back to sleep, not before. Only then did we sleep the peaceful, happy, virtuous sleep of the faithful, confident that "God helps those who help themselves."

Yes, for us during our time in Mississippi, mosquitoes were practically a religion.

Believe me.

Smooth? Sailing

I don't know who coined the expression "smooth sailing," but I do know it wasn't any sailor.

I've been sailing four times, all paid-lessons off Hilton Head Island when I was in my teens. My family's custom was to take a one-week beach vacation every summer, and my father liked to schedule some special activity to make the week memorable. It's been about 45 years since I took the lessons, and I have to admit, I've never forgot.

On the first day of sailing school, I was told that I'd be going solo, which meant there'd be no instructor in the boat, only 5 other teenagers, a couple of whom had sailed a little before. I wondered since they were paying for lessons just as I was, why they'd be considered qualified teachers, and it seemed to me that going solo would be more appropriately scheduled for the end of the week, not on my very first day. Imagine if you signed up for, say, welding lessons and on your first day you were told you'd be using a powerful acetylene torch without an actual teacher present. "Here's the torch. Here's the metal. Have fun!" That's how I felt.

I and the 5 other kids in our small sailboat were towed through a channel and then released into Calibogue Sound. Calibogue Sound? More like Calibogue *Un*sound. You see, as we sailed with the wind, we got closer and closer to leaving the sound and entering the open Atlantic Ocean. We tried to turn the boat around several times, but it didn't work. The technical description for our failure was that the boat didn't "jibe." I'll tell you what didn't jibe—paying money for a lesson and then being abandoned to die in the open sea. That's what didn't fucking jibe. Finally, one of the other teens remembered we had to pull up the center board to turn, so I survived to a second lesson.

The next day, there was an adult qualified sailing instructor in the boat, which gave me hope I'd have a less life-threatening experience this time. The teacher said that the breezy weather was ideal; we were in for a real treat. What I learned on this second day is that what's meant by "ideal sailing" is the situation in which the boat is on its edge at about, I'd say, an 80 degree angle to the water such that it is just about to flip over. For an analogy, imagine you drove your car around a corner so fast that 2 tires lifted off the pavement and that observers then told you, "Now that is some ideal driving. Don't you feel exhilarated? Don't you feel free?" I felt free all right. Free to drown in Calibogue Sound. Free to be eaten by sharks. Free to swim back to shore, if I could make it, and hike my drenched ass back to the rental house.

At first as we were careening through the sound, I was on the low side of the boat, which meant my head was only inches from dipping into the water. I thought I'd much prefer to be on the high side—until I actually was. On the high side, I was about 10 feet up in the air. We high-siders had to hook our feet and lean our bodies out as far as we could as human ballast. The higher we went, the more we had to stretch out and lean back. If we flipped, low-siders would enter the water first, but we high-siders had a lot farther to fall.

When I showed up for my fourth lesson, I was told that I'd be going (Oh, joy!) solo again. On this day we were not towed through the narrow channel between the marina and the sound even though the wind was blowing directly toward us, which meant we had to perform a technique known as tacking. "Tacking" essentially means zigzagging, which takes longer and requires a lot more work than sailing in a straight line. Tacking involves coordinated pulling of ropes (or "sheets" as sailors insanely call them) to move the jib sail so that it catches enough wind to pull the boat from the zig direction to the zag direction. If you don't pull the ropes fast enough, you lose the wind, fail to have enough speed to turn or what's called "come about," and you end up stuck on the bank in the Goddamn stinking mud for like the tenth time. The boat didn't come about. And I'll tell you what else didn't come about—any desire to ever again risk the muck-sticking, death-threatening fiasco that some people with sick senses of humor sadistically call "sailing." That's what by God didn't come about.

My father had paid for me to have 5 lessons, but when the fifth day arrived, I let that little opportunity just sail on by.

Saladmaster Disaster

When Renae, a graduate student that both my wife and I had taught, repeatedly begged us to attend a fried-chicken-dinner Saladmaster sales pitch at her apartment, we finally relented. We'd get a free meal with no obligations, and she would get some free knives as a hostess gift—an unbeatable deal for everybody, Renae said.

Renae, her husband, and four children lived in an efficiency apartment. Right away I felt good that we were helping her family get those much-needed utensils. The kitchen was tiny—about the area of a king-sized bed. In the bed with us were three other customer couples (all strangers), the eight folding chairs we sat on, our cook, his wife, and of course the stove. Once the stove was going, the bed got pretty hot.

When our cook/Saladmaster salesman began his hour-long infomercial, it dawned on me that I should have done more research The name "Saladmaster" had made me think we'd be asked to buy a plastic salad spinner, maybe a $20 item, or perhaps a food processor for shredding lettuce that would cost no more than a hundred bucks. But Saladmaster was actually a company that sold premium quality pot and pan sets costing in the neighborhood of 700 to a thousand dollars—a neighborhood I didn't visit too often. I started feeling anxious and claustrophobic.

I don't think our cook literally had that perspiring disease, but as the cooking progressed, his forehead got sweatier and sweatier. Meanwhile, his silent assistant-wife did a semi-convincing job of appearing semi-cheerful.

Since Saladmaster pans were double-walled stainless steel, much of the sales strategy was to convince us just how awful the cheaper pans we probably owned were. Aluminum pans were especially targeted. Saladmaster

Man heated some water in an old dented, stained, pock-marked aluminum sauce pan, let it cool, then passed it around with a tablespoon and directed us to see for ourselves just how horribly the aluminum contaminated the taste. I watched as my wife dipped the spoon, brought it to her lips, made a face, and then passed to me. I have to admit that SM Man was right: the water *did* taste metallic, bitter, and foul. Later, when I asked the woman who took me for better or worse (I think you can tell which she got)—when I asked her about the taste, she said, "*I* didn't drink it; I just pretended. Did you actually drink it? You idiot, why would you *do* that?"

After the meal, we had to wait our turns to be pressured as individual couples in a closed-door room. My wife and I were the last couple, and SM Man was in a bad mood from the start. I told him that I was glad to hear such good things about double-walled stainless steel cookware since my parents had given us a set of Belgique only the Christmas before. Our host said he'd never heard of Belgique. My wife and I felt sorry for him, so we offered to buy a chef's knife we didn't need, but the pitchman, maybe out of disgust or a sense of defeat, seemed uninterested in such a small sale.

Later, Renae told us that none of the four couples had bought anything and that the Saladmaster Man had refused to give Renae even the minimum guaranteed hostess gift on the grounds that one of the couples wasn't married.

So nobody got anything they wanted. Except me: I got an absolutely free, unforgettable meal in cramped, hot quarters among stranger bedfellows and a sweaty, desperate host—a free two-course dinner of piping-hot, delicious big helpings of bad feelings and guilt.

Socks on the Lam

In the last 40 years, I've never lost a single sock. Ever. Maybe losing socks is your Achilles heel, but don't let anyone pull the wool over your eyes; it doesn't have to be. Instead, pad along in *my* footsteps.

Step number one: Whenever a pair of socks is not on your feet or in a laundry appliance, roll the tops together enough that the two socks will stay paired. Every. Single. Time. I sometimes wear socks to bed, and if my feet get too hot in the middle of the night, even though I'm half asleep, I still pair them as I remove them. Possible issues can arise, but they're rare. Once I awoke with only one sock on. The other sock had been stolen by the foot of my bed. That's what I said—the *foot* of my bed.

Step two is a little more complex but also more fun since this is your opportunity to hone your detective skills.

To best clean your socks, you'll want to unpair them as you put them in the washer, so this is when you're most vulnerable to sock loss. Yes, there's many a slip between the washer and dryer. As a matter of course, always double check the washer. You should also familiarize yourself with every hidey hole in your laundry room so you know where to look first when a sock goes on the lam. My escape artists most often hunker down between the two appliances or between one of them and the wall.

Once, when I used a powerful front-loading laundromat washer, I discovered a sock clinging to the almost-impossible-to-see *top* of the drum. I had to squat down and look up inside the washer. (Two of my briefs were also stuck up there, but that's another story—"Where Oh Where Is My Underwear?")

I highly recommend that you fold your laundry right away so that your memory is sharp. I have found socks hiding inside pants legs, inside the sleeves of long-sleeved shirts, and inside the corner "pockets" of fitted bedsheets. You need to be able to remember what clothing you've already hung up or put away so you know whom to interrogate. If you suspect your wife's clingy skirt of complicity, just say, "Ma'm, are you perhaps harboring a fugitive?" If she appears uncooperative, you may have to pat her down—if you're feeling frisky.

During the missing-socks portion of this process, it's crucial to feel confident. You must believe in yourself and take pride in your sock-retention abilities. Your mantra must be "I am *not* a loser. I am *not* a loser." Remember that no fast getaway car or helicopter is going to get involved, and, really, how far can your sock get on foot?

You should be able to run it down even if it's athletic.

Once when I lived in an apartment building with a community laundry room, I ended up back at my apartment with a sock missing its mate. I retraced my path and searched every likely cranny, but no luck. Then I remembered that an impatient neighbor had removed my laundry from the dryer and put it in my basket. Since I am not a loser, that meant my neighbor was the loser. I knocked on her door and asked, "By any chance do you have my sock mixed in with your laundry? It's a blue crew with a gold toe." Though my words were polite, I believe my tone conveyed, "I know you have my sock. I want it back." In a minute she returned and remanded the abetted footwear back into my custody.

The single life is no life for a sock. They should be mated for life. When one goes missing, I don't rest until I track it down. I'm Bill Spencer. Sock detective.

Join me, and never be a loser again.

A Scene from the Movie of My Life

I've long thought that movies have an advantage over real life partly because of the soundtracks—the perfect music to help you feel exactly what you're supposed to feel in the cinematic moment—and partly because the director is able to draw your attention to what's most important to notice.

But once, I did have an experience that *seemed* like a film scene.

A former college colleague of mine asked me one afternoon to play hooky from my office hours to help him with a pressing errand. Now, I taught for 31 years, and I *never* skipped out on even one office hour—except this once. So at the outset here we have a *Ferris Bueller's Day Off* kind of setup. Cue the music.

This former friend (I'll call him Bob) was remodeling his house and needed to move and store a large, round-topped solid oak table. He explained to me that the table was an heirloom, in his wife's family for several generations, and his wife—who had an incendiary temper according to what Bob had said many, many times—had insisted that he rent a storage unit and move the table there until the construction work was finished so that there was not even the slightest danger that it could be damaged. Just moving the table to the side and covering it with pads was not sufficient; the table was far too precious to take such a risk. So it's clear that in this movie frame, the director was careful to focus my attention on how important the table was and how temperamental Bob's wife was. I think music from *The Godfather* would work here, or, abandoning subtlety, perhaps the theme from *Jaws*.

Bob was already unhappy about the cost of the storage unit, and to avoid any further moving cost, he had borrowed an old pickup truck from another colleague and of course had recruited me.

Our first job was to unscrew the table top from its pedestal base, a massive center column that branched out at the bottom into four side supports. Some ominous violin screeching would be appropriate at the moment we separated the top from its base.

We moved the base into the truck first and then carefully loaded the round top onto some cushioning blankets. I noticed that the truck bed was wide enough that the table would have fit even if we had not removed the base. But it was not wide enough for the top to lie flat. So we propped the top upright on its edge. When Bob went to shut the tailgate, it clanked but didn't catch. [At this point the camera zooms in on a sizable rusty dent at the top of the tailgate near the latching mechanism.] Bob's second try also failed, but the third time worked, and we were set to go. All safe and secure.

One thing I love about well-done movies is that when big plot points unfold, there's both true surprise and also a sense of inevitability, a sense that of *course* that's what happened; that's what *had* to happen.

Bob started the truck and turned on the radio. I think Blood, Sweat, & Tears' "Spinning Wheel" was playing. Bob drove slowly and cautiously and I was enjoying the music when I heard some metallic percussion that I didn't remember in the song, followed by a loud thud behind us. I turned my head. [Closeup on Bob's eyes in the rearview mirror, then a wide shot on what he sees: the tabletop rolling down the middle of the residential street behind us. You can even *hear* it rolling. The song on the radio switches to Creedence Clearwater Revival and the tempo triples: "Big wheel keep on turnin'. . . . Rollin', rollin', rollin' down the highway."] I might be a little hazy on the lyrics. Anyway, I watched with bugged-out eyes and open mouth as the table rolled perfectly for about half a block. I couldn't believe how far it got, and then it stalled and started to wobble-roll on its edge faster and faster in a tight circle the way a spun quarter or coaster or hula hoop will, until it whirred to a stop.

Bob backed up to get the news regarding his future. We saw that the entire edge of the table looked as if it had been sanded. It was rough and was lighter in color than the rest of the top. But otherwise the table was OK. Bob said, "I can fix this. I'll sneak out nights to the storage unit and smooth and re-stain this and nobody," meaning his wife, "will ever know what happened."

I don't know if Bob succeeded in his optimistic assessment or not. I was already an accomplice to the crime and didn't want to be an accomplice to the coverup. So I never asked. Was his Mission Impossible?

Cue the music. Fade to black.

Marketing Your Screenplay

After I retired from teaching college English, I wrote a screenplay and realized a dream. When I tried to market the screenplay, I realized a nightmare.

The script, "Angel Pays a Visit," is a comedy. My attempts to market it have been a comedy, too. When I completed it almost six years ago, I envisioned that getting it made into a big-budget, popular, Oscar-winning film would require a lot of time printing and binding copies and mailing them out to interested buyers. So far the number of requests for a copy is zero.

In my experience, you have to *pay* people to read your screenplay. Even then, only contest judges and critique services will read it. Studio executives are prohibited by their lawyers from reading scripts unless you sign a 20-page release saying you will not sue the studio if they steal your work. Several studios returned my one-page query letters with notices that they were "unread." One envelope came back with "Return to Sender" scribbled on it. It had been opened but not resealed.

Following the advice of one of my books, I went to see a former departmental colleague, who taught screenwriting, during his scheduled office hour. He said I was too old and that I'd wasted my time. "You've aged out," he said. He made it clear he thought I was wasting *his* time as well. When I asked him if he'd give me some feedback on my query letter, he said, "No, that wouldn't be a good use of my time." He did, however, have time (10 minutes) to complain of his own script-marketing frustrations.

After the heartening talk with my generous colleague, I bought the latest *Hollywood Screenwriting Directory* and marked which companies preferred comedies and would also accept unsolicited query emails from nobodies like me.

I sent out 80 emails and received 4 responses, all declining my offer of additional information. My favorite response, and the fastest, indicated I was going about marketing all wrong, but to my good fortune the responder had written a book that would teach me correct tactics and deliver "outsized results"—available from Amazon for just $13.88.

What I did instead of buying still another book was to list my script for 6 months with a searchable screenplay database service. Finally, "Angel Pays a Visit" would be available to producers actively wanting to buy a script. The first company to take a look was not Disney, or 20th Century Fox, or Warner Brothers, or even MGM; it was Kranky. And "Kranky" is a pretty good description of how I felt. Other companies that glanced before passing included Inflammable Films, Lemon Fresh Bastards, and Gimme A Break. I agree: Gimme A Break.

I obviously need to do some significant revision—not of my script, but of my life. Taking my cue from screenwriting books, I've decided to move to L.A., take an entry-level job with a film studio, and erase 40 years from my age.

Maybe my next screenplay will be about time travel.

Jesus Does Stand-Up

The Apostles all kept telling him he needed to lighten up, he was running off potential converts with the heavy sermonizing, so he decided to try stand-up.

Once the crowd was sitting around the top of the hill, he started riffing on the Bible, said he was writing a book but confessed he had a ghost writer, then hit 'em with the punch—*a HOLY Ghost writer* and the little drummer boy gave him a Ba-Dum-Bump! Said he was working on a sequel to the OLD testament but needed help coming up with a title, he was open to suggestions.

Then he segued to a set on sin, called *original sin* an oxymoron, kept punctuating his patter with a high falsetto impression in an Egyptian accent, saying, *The DEV-il made me do it!*

Then he got more personal, poked fun at his situation, said he didn't get no respect, said, *I'm the Son of God and they've got me making coffee tables,* said his mother couldn't even describe his father to him, a one-night stand, dark, and she never really saw Him, she mainly remembered talking to His wing-man. An invisible father and to make matters worse He was tri-polar, said he was healthier than his father, half-man, half-God, so he was only *bi*-polar, another rimshot on the drum, and the crowd was really tickled by now, said he never closed doors because he really WAS born in a barn, said he was surrounded by asses when he was born—*and there were a few farm animals, too*, he said. The crowd was on the ropes.

What was the deal with the magi? he said. *Who gives myrrh as a baby gift? Or frankincense? I mean how wise could they be? How'd they even GET a reputation for being wise? It probably didn't hurt that they were—KINGS!*

People were almost rolling down the hill now they were laughing so hard, some rocking forward, some slapping their legs, some with tears and blowing their noses.

He let 'em laugh till they were all laughed out, then said, *But seriously, folks—love one another.*

My time's up, he said. *Thanks for listening. Thanks for laughing. You've been a great crowd.* And he asked them to watch for his book and then he said, *I'm Jesus Christ. Tell your friends. I'll be here all week.*

Garden & Gun

When my sister-in-law visited recently, she brought the latest issue of the magazine *Garden & Gun.* Yes, that's what I said—*Garden & Gun.* And while this pairing might at first seem the teeniest bit unlikely, the magazine has been around since 2007 and now boasts over a million readers. When I thought about that level of success, it dawned on me that Americans regard guns as something like bacon and cheese: everything can be made better by adding them. Who wants a plain old bun-and-patty garden mag when you can have a bacon cheeseburger? Almost nobody. So because of America's nearly insatiable appetite for "bacon and cheese," I propose the creation of several new magazines published on the model of *Garden & Gun.* Why not tap into what is clearly a much bigger market?

A smart first step would be to create similar spin-offs of *Garden & Gun,* such as *Stamen & Pistol, Hollyhocks & Handguns,* or *Guns 'n' Roses.* This last one could be packaged with a bonus music CD.

Then several brand new markets could be "targeted."

Run & Gun—"For the Active Shooter." Jogging down a street is boring. But jogging down a street with an assault rifle—now *that's* interesting!

Camera & Gun—"How to Shoot Wildlife." Filled with tips on capturing the perfect image of beautiful fauna right before popping a cap in its ass. Tie-in possible with a new product: a rifle with a barrel-mounted camera that doubles as the scope; the trigger would also snap the pic. This function would be touted as the "snapshot" feature. So many possibilities here I shutter to think.

K-9's & M-16's—"For Lovers of Dogs and Destruction."
Semper Fido.

Horse & Trigger—"Shooting's Even More Fun When You're Mounted." Catering to cowboys, cowgirls, cavalry, mounties, Roy Rogers fans, and fans of both kinds of Colts.

Women & Weapons. No subtitle needed. This magazine could have a sister publication, *Victoria's Secret Arsenal*—"Lingerie and Lasers." So revealing that half the magazine will be redacted, but only the weaponry portion will be *top* secret, thus filling the niche being vacated by the now-nudeless *Playboy.*

Kitchen & Kalashnikov—"Killer Menus and Killer Men."

Sweat & Bullets—"Exercise Your Body AND Your 2nd-Amendment Rights." The title is something every American can identify with.

Finally, established magazines that already have name recognition can build on their reputations and increase subscriptions and sales with just a few tiny tweaks. For example, *Time* magazine could devote more coverage to mass and accidental shootings and retitle itself *Time & Time Again.*
Herewith some other possibilities:

U.S. News & *Loud* **Report**
Life *& Death*
Look *& Shoot*
Poets *& Fighters*
MAD, *Armed, & Dangerous*
AA_RP_**G**
Oxford American *Sniper*
Field & *Scream*

People & *Other Targets*

If I haven't missed my guess, this *Garden & Gun* concept has marketing potential that can only be described as explosive. America is clamoring for "more bacon and cheese, please," and who can blame us? After all, who doesn't want a magazine that's—fully loaded?

I Killed Mr. Lincoln

There's a joke that a British gardener left a suicide note of a single word—clay. If I told the joke, the punchline would be "roses."

Imagine you have a beloved 98-year-old grandmother. Let's call her Rose. She needs extensive surgery every winter, nearly round-the-clock attentive care all year long, and you know that whatever you do, pretty soon she's going to die. Do you really want to take on that level of heart-rending care giving?

I have so far watched more than 20 grannies waste away from diseases like black spot, sooty mold, and fireblight or be devoured more quickly by aphids, rose chafers, slugs, and Japanese beetles.

I don't buy roses anymore. But I wasn't always so wise.

When my wife decided she wanted roses in our Mississippi Delta backyard, we bought landscape timbers, ordered half of a dump truck load of topsoil, constructed a 30-foot-long raised bed, and ordered and planted a dozen Simplicity roses. We envisioned that our roses would live up to their name and that soon we'd have a gorgeous hedge of pink profusion. The roses did in fact fulfill the promise of their name—Simplicity. Within two years they were all dead and no longer required any care. What could be simpler than that?

We signed up for more heartache after that by trying tea roses: French Lace, Double Delight, Tropicana, and my favorite of favorites, Mr. Lincoln. I bought an extensive arsenal of chemical weapons and even went out every summer night in the sweltering, mosquito-swarming Delta dark to hand pick scores of rose chafers—or rose *chompers* as I called them—off of our dear dying relatives. To no avail. After blooming once or twice, they all died. Yes, I had killed Mr. Lincoln. I had two more Mr. Lincolns after that, and you can guess what happened. It's a lot to bear—three assassinations.

We gave up on roses for several years, until we moved to the mountains of North Carolina, where roses, we thought, would surely find a more welcoming environment. We bought a Peace rose, a beautiful, fragrant, award-winning flower. Or at least that's what it's supposed to be. No, our Peace rose isn't dead yet. Even after ten years it's still alive—if you can call a single short cane, almost completely denuded, "alive." She looks like she *wants* to die, but I just don't have the heart to help her on her way. There's no avoiding the fact that soon she'll be—in the ground. We tell her it's OK to go; she doesn't have to suffer anymore. But she still clings.

If I can give you just one piece of advice, it's this: Don't fall in love with roses.

If you do fall in love, you're in for a world of hurt. And you will never have any Peace.

Coffin Shoppin'

Coffin shoppin' is a grave undertaking. It can be confusing and inconvenient even though there's never so far been even one complaint from an end-consumer. My fervent hope is that one day every mall will have a boutique shoppe—Dead, Death, & Beyond.

I acquired some expertise in this process some years ago when in the span of three months, my mother and both of my wife's parents shuffled off their mortal coils in what one family member characterized as Death Race 2013. It quickly became apparent that coffins are expensive and that it's difficult to find out how much they cost. Funeral-home brochures with images of specific models do not usually show the cost. The funeral home "showroom" models also offer no hint of such crass monetary considerations. Costs are instead indicated on a separate list, for the sake of making it easier, I'm sure, to quickly lower the prices for After-Christmas and Day-of-the-Dead Sales.

The cheapest funeral option, and one that will additionally earn you sainthood, is to donate your body to medical science, as my dear friend Dorothy did when she died. Most companies that guide you through body donation offer free cremation. One such service, MedCure, additionally offers, at no charge, scattering your ashes at sea. Even if you weren't in the military, this way you can have a stately marine corpse send-off.

If you're not saintly or are squeamish about your mortal remains becoming a medical school commodity, your next cheapest option is standard cremation, but beware: crematoria may still try to sell you an expensive wood coffin rather than the least-expensive, most practical way to go—a sturdy cardboard box.

If you have an ingrained fear of after-life blazing heat or don't die on board a ship, you're going to need a coffin. But take heart. There are still nontraditional ways you can save on coffin costs.

One innovative option is the rental casket. Yes, I said "rental." Rental caskets are perfect when you want one for show but not for go. These expensive-looking rentals contain plain box inserts that you have to buy. By law these liner boxes prevent the body from touching the casket. After the public ceremonies, the hinged casket end is let down and the insert is easily slid out. According to www.cremation.com, the average casket rental is $750-$900 with purchase of the insert adding another $150-$250.

Another ingenious strategy is to buy dual-purpose coffin furniture from such companies as Final Furniture Limited. The best-known version of this is the bookcase coffin made from wood or metal. Nature's Casket offers pine boxes for $610-$710, to which book shelves can be added for another $100. Other companies provide even more furniture options. Chuck Lakin, based in Maine, designs coffins that can easily be converted from beds, bookcases, or chests of drawers—as low as $400 and all less than $1,000. Why *not* rest in a bed that will become your eternal resting place? Who doesn't want a coffin coffee table? What a lovely hope chest one would make for a soon-to-be bride. And if you buy the bookcase model, you can shelve classics from Faulkner, Agee, and Ernest J. Gaines: *As I Lay Dying*, *A Death in the Family*, and *A Lesson before Dying*. (If your body's going to be burned, you don't need a bookcase coffin; what you need then, I guess, is a Kindle.)

This double-duty strategy has also given birth to annual coffin races, such as the ones in Denton, Texas, or Manitou Springs, Colorado. Some of these coffin racers are wheeled but not motorized, as in a soapbox derby, while others involve four running pall bearers carrying a (live) lightweight youngster in a box. Sprinting pall bearers? Is anyone appalled? How do they prepare? Do they re-hearse? The coffin racers in Elmore, Ohio's Tombstone Derby are often built around riding mowers—designed to mow down the competition, I suppose. (How are they paying for these contraptions? With second morgue-ages?) Yes, this sport puts the "fun" in "funeral." And it gives new meaning to the phrase "reaching the finish line." I don't know if any coffin races have ever resulted in driver deaths, but if they did, just think of the convenience.

Even if you don't fancy a coffin to shelve your hardbacks in or one you could trim your lawn with—if, in other words, you want an old-fashioned single-purpose burial box—you can still save money and still express your individuality. My mother, who was very concerned that her final resting vessel look "feminine," concentrated her showroom shopping on white or pink caskets decorated with floral images. There is, unfortunately, some sales pressure under these circumstances since it's so hard to say, "No thanks, I'm just looking."

One way to avoid this pressure is to buy your coffin online from a company such as bestpricecaskets.com, which repeatedly reassures shoppers, "Funeral homes must accept our caskets" because of Federal Trade Commission law. Best Price Caskets seems to live up to its name. Scores of models in metal or wood are offered at prices from $795 (18 gauge steel) to $2995 (copper or bronze). The savings over funeral-home prices are substantial, especially for top-shelf merchandise. Of particular interest, this company offers six models with a mossy-oak camouflage lining, the benefits of which are obvious. After all, who wants to face death any more clearly or directly than necessary? The more camouflage the better, I'd say. Dressing your deceased loved one in his or her favorite camo clothing would complete the effect. "I thought Uncle John was supposed to be in this coffin. Where did he disappear to?"

Of course with an online purchase, there is the issue of delivery to consider. Best Price Caskets promises free ground shipping that takes 5-12 days. However, most customers, the company notes, opt for next-day air shipping that typically adds $300-$350 to the cost for those who live close to a major airport. You can show up at the airport yourself and throw your purchase in the back of your pickup truck, or it can be delivered to you by a "Hot-Shot Courier." I'm not sure exactly what a Hot-Shot Courier is, but I sure do like the sound of it.

The coffin business has clearly made real strides in offering options that allow shoppers to save money, to get double duty from what has in the past been a single-use product, and to express their individual personalities—but for my money they haven't yet gone far enough. The images I saw of coffin racers got me thinking about the logical next step—coffins that look like the deceased's favorite car—or when burial space is not an issue, perhaps the actual car itself. (Remember the Munsters' drag racer named "Dragula"?) And cars will work whether the customer prefers burial or cremation.

Me? I want to be sent off in style behind the wheel of my appropriately black 1997 Firebird. I want a coffin that's got some miles on it, one that's got a few dents and dings—just like I do. Fill the tank with premium gasoline. Start up Lenny Kravitz's "I Want to Fly Away" on the sound system. Have Vikings shoot flaming arrows from a far distance, and watch as I go out in a blaze of glory, watch as my Firebird takes one last trip and flies me to the unknown world beyond.

And the Firebird is already paid for.

Dead-People Trees

Of the many innovative human burial concepts I'm aware of, the one that interests me most right now is the method of turning your corpse into a tree.

A concept by Anna Citelli and Raoul Bretzel called Capsula Mundi envisions trees growing from decomposing burial pods. Trees or tree seeds would be planted on top of a corpse in fetal position encased in a biodegradable egg-shaped pod. Citelli and Bretzel hope that some day cemeteries with headstones will be replaced with entire forests of dead-people trees.

Doesn't this seem a fitting way to commemorate a person's entire his-tree? Wouldn't such symbolism constitute a kind of po-e-tree?

Instead of deciding whether to have a coffin made of oak, cherry, or walnut, you could decide which of these trees you'd like to *become.*

Imagine all the opportunities of suiting the tree to the person: for prickly people, spiky locust trees; for offbeat relatives, nuts; for the nicest people, real peaches and plums; for rich women, firs; and for bonded couples who die at the same time, a single pear. Was the person a misanthrope, a sourpuss? Imagine his delight at becoming a hackberry, mulberry, or Chinese cherry; having birds eat his fruit; and then crapping all over people's cars. Wouldn't that just make his eternal day?

Maybe you died forgotten and alone, but with this technique, even in death it's not too late for you to become poplar.

I myself think I'd like to become a fruit tree, say an apple—a sweet apple tree so that people would say, "Bill's bark is worse than his bite." Though dead, I'd still be fruitful. I could become a pie, a cobbler, or a strudel. Why,

I could fritter away the afterlife. Though decomposing, I could still have a peel. I could be saucy. I could be hard apple cider and be as intoxicating as ever. I could work on my core. And I'd still be in people's lives: An apple a day keeps Bill Spencer in play. I could symbolically say, "Eat me!" And anyone who did would be guilty of can-apple-ism. As an apple tree, I think I could continue to grow—as a person—if I apple-ied myself. I think I could really flower. And once I was established, I could branch out. Every spring my sap would rise, and every autumn I'd get more colorful.

And I'd try to get my wife to become an apple tree, too, planted as nearby as possible. We could spend our whole deaths together. She'd continue to be the apple of my eye. I could be a Gala, and she could be my Honeycrisp. Both apples but with our distinct differences. Two varieties of the same fruit. And I'd be very, very happy because even after we're dead, we could still cross-pollinate.

Brief Anecdotes

The Anecdotes Not Taken

According to their website, *Reader's Digest* prints only about 250 of the 250,000 humor submissions they receive each year. Below are items I submitted that were among the 249,750 not taken.

Introduction

I have a reputation for joking around. When my mother attended a ceremony at my high school, I went up to her afterwards, stuck out my hand, and introduced myself. She played along and shook my hand. Seconds later when a classmate came over, I introduced her to him: "This is my mother." He laughed and said, "No she's not. I just saw you introduce yourself. You can't fool me."

Not a Joke

We consider humor a serious art in my family. A friend who prided himself on his own comedic talent felt unappreciated when my five-year-old stepson didn't laugh at some of his wordplay. "Didn't you like my joke?" he asked. "It wasn't a joke," my stepson replied; "it was a pun."
"Well, did you like my pun, then?"
"I've heard better."

Easter Egg-centric

At my stepson's third-grade Open House, the teacher called me over to the bulletin board decorated with student-drawn Easter eggs. She gestured to all the traditional pastel-colored eggs with a smile, then pointed disapprovingly to a macabrely deviant oval—half red and half black, with horns on it. "Here's *your* son's," she said. When I looked to my stepson, he smiled and explained, "It's a deviled egg."

I've never been prouder.

Police School

When the subject of a possible career in law enforcement came up, I warned my 12-year-old stepson, "Police work is boring most of the time, and then every once in a while, someone takes a shot at you." "Oh," he said, "it's like school."

A Real Lulu

Students at my university who signed up for a theater-tour-of-London class received a crash course in vocabulary differences between American and British English: Bobby for police officer, bonnet for car hood, tube for subway, and loo for toilet. One student who was lost and looking for the nearest underground train station got a surprised stare when she asked a Londoner, "Can you tell me how to get on the loo?"

Just Married

After being on FaceBook for two years, my friend finally noticed the place in his profile for "Relationship Status," so he checked "Married." Almost immediately there was a flood of inquiries from friends and a "What's going on?" confrontation from his wife of 46 years. FaceBook had posted the update "Married Today."

Where in the World?

When a world-traveling friend called to tell me he was in the area and would like to get together, I asked him where he was. He said, "Eur-AW-phus." Since I could think of no nearby town that sounded anything like this, I stalled with smalltalk, then asked again, "Where did you say you were?" The reply was the same—"Eur-AW-phus." So I resorted to subtle, clever probing: "What's that near?" Finally, he gave me more context: "I'm on campus—at your office."

Attention Getter

At the university where I worked, the faculty sponsor of Sigma Tau Delta honor society sent an email inviting us to note the upcoming initiation date with this subject line: "STD Alert."

"Aye, There's the Rub!"

In my family, birthday mishaps are legendary. For my brother's sixteenth birthday my mother baked him a cake, covered it with homemade frosting, and then to personalize the cake with my brother's interests, she used a store-bought tube of icing to outline a Bible and a tennis racket. When she checked the cake later, however, the drawings had disappeared. Baffled, she redecorated, but once again the icing sank down into the frosting. She then inspected the red and white tube of "icing" and realized that what she'd actually been topping the cake with was my father's tube of Deep Heating Rub.

Electrifying Puns

Electric companies aren't usually known for their sense of humor, but on my electric bill, the total amount due appears after the words "current charges."

Thanks for the Memory

When my wife's dad needed V.A. Benefits, his memory was gone and she couldn't find his Marine serial number. Her V.A. contact suggested she march up to her dad and say, "Soldier! Name, rank, and serial number!" It worked. Without hesitation he barked out the number she needed.

The Sun Also Rises

My wife, Carolyn, learned a lot on an Outward Bound hike along Washington's Olympic coast, but a New York City debutante in her group learned even more. As Carolyn led the hike, the deb asked how she knew the direction they were going. When my wife explained how she took bearings from the ocean to the west and from the location of the sun, the deb wondered how the sun could be of any help since its position was constantly changing. Carolyn explained, "Of course, it rises in the east."

"The sun rises in the east?" the deb asked.

"Yes."

"Every day?"

Regal Legals

I heard former Mississippi governor Ronnie Musgrove tell the story of his very first class at Ole Miss's School of Law. Nervous and full of self-doubts, he arrived ridiculously early, talked to another first-day law student already there, and decided, "I'll do fine. I'm a lot more qualified to be here than *this* guy."

That other guy, who filled Musgrove with such a sense of superiority and confidence, turned out to be John Grisham.

How Long IS a Boyfriend?

"I've learned that boyfriends are a unit of time now," my co-worker announced. "When I asked my daughter something, she indicated how out of touch I was by saying, 'Oh, Dad, that was three boyfriends ago.'"

Too Hot to Handle

When my 80-year-old mother was evaluating job applications, she bragged she had immediately rejected one since the applicant wasn't of good character. When I asked her how she knew, she said, "His email address is @hotmail. I'm not naive. I know what *that* means."

Foiled Again

One of my freshmen asked me, "Would you please *print* the notes you put on the board? I can't read curses."

Strange Coincidence?

One of my struggling high school classmates, musing on an upcoming move, announced, "I came here two years ago, and now after two years I'm leaving. Seems like everything's happening in two years."

Into the Mouth of Babes

When my niece, aged two, swallowed her gum, she announced, "Mommy, my gum went down my drain!"

Son to the Rescue

Some years ago my wife was mortified when in response to her asking about room availability, a hotel clerk dismissively said, "Our rooms *start* at $200 a night. Then her techie son stepped in: "Do your rooms have Wi-Fi?" The clerk's expression brightened, and he gushed, "No, but we're getting it soon."

"Let's go, Mom," her champion said. "We don't want to stay *here*."

Bill Spencer

I Upped MY Translation Skills

When my wife noticed the Chinese calligraphy artwork on a friend's wall, he told her the three characters translated as "When the sun rises over the beautiful mountain, it casts a long shadow." My wife, who's studied Chinese, had to disagree: "What it actually says is "Up you (possessive)"—or, in other words, "Up yours."

Unclear on the Concept

One evening, the local news coverage of a government agency's loss of funds included an interview with a man on the street, who said, "They lost thousands of dollars and don't know where it is. I don't lose a dollar that I don't know where it is."

Is That a Recommendation?

Asked to write a recommendation letter for an intelligent but remarkably lazy student, one college professor struggled until he hit upon this honest assessment: "You'll be so lucky if you get her to work for you."

Fightin' Words

On visits to my mother I typically could get through only one or two days before some seemingly inevitable friction occurred. Before one visit I vowed to my wife, "No conflict for the *whole* visit this time!" Though I always arrived after a five-hour drive at about 3:00 p.m. and though I'd already told her to expect me at the usual time, I decided to call before leaving (at 10:00 a.m.) just to say I was right on schedule. I thought, "This extra courtesy will get the visit off on the right foot."

When I told her, she said, "What?! You haven't left yet?! I thought you'd be here by now."

Grade-School Gourmand

When my well-traveled seven-year-old stepson ordered bison in a Santa Fe restaurant, I smiled in amusement and waited expectantly to see his reaction. What would he think of this exotic new dish? After his first bite, I asked, "How's your bison?"

He said, "I've had better."

Good Question!

After presenting a science museum lecture on dinosaurs, my adult stepson asked his audience of children if there were any questions. One little boy raised his hand. His question?

"I have a trampoline."

Student Bloopers

Super Duper Student Bloopers

I collected all of the following sentences and items from students in my college English composition courses over a 31-year teaching career. Most of the humor comes from sound-alike word confusions, typos, or misspellings. Our very rich language sometimes makes for a little fun.

Can anybody have ESP, or does it run in your *jeans*?

She hates the ocean and water unless she has her *googles*.

Trouble was always just around the *coroner*.

Descartes found that there is doubt in almost every *faucet* of life.

If the attorney *flea*-bargains for money, he will do an injustice to his client.

On the way to the door I stubbed my toe, so as I met him for the first time, I stood there *thriving* in pain.

On my trip to Alaska, the change of *climax* really threw my body out of *wax*.

The only bad thing about getting around by foot is walking in *blistery* cold weather.

The drunk's unmanageable hairs were tangled all over his *discarded* head.

The majority of my fifth grade year was filled with rejection, hate, and anger. I was ostracized from most of the *clichés*.

Walking to a seat is like walking through a *mind* field.

I was grateful for the values that my parents *installed* in me.

We were arrested, but luckily we took only enough value to be charged with *mister miner* felony.

That year he grew more than a foot *tall* from his spine being straightened.

Some people will go to extreme *links* to get what they want.

As we walked down every *isle*, my feet became *exalted*, but we moved along.

Connie is also a person with a head on her shoulders.

The university could explain registration and financial aid procedures in more *debt*.

Today we are so in-*depth* because of all the money we spend on materialistic things.

Many explain that the advantage of credit is that one can make a major *purpose* and spread the payments for it across several months.

In some cases it is the company's fault for issuing a credit card to an *illegitimate* person.

I just expected and deserved a *sanity* restroom.

I wanted to make *a mince* for being a jerk.

Kentucky Fried Chicken has always been known for its finger *looking* good chicken.

It came with a bag of French fries and a *bowel* of cooked vegetables.

At the Magnolia Bar, you can also purchase a *picture* of draft beer for four dollars and twenty-five cents.

The salads and salad bar have many different assortments that *thick* out in your mind.

The other food items that freegans consume, such as fruits and vegetables, are usually in their *ripper* stage, yet still good to eat.

This girl is awkward to meet. Her *aneurisms* are jerky and disconnected at times, but she is an absolute joy to know.

The Residence Director explained that I needed to stay out of trouble because if I got caught underage drinking again I could face *explosion*.

I tore the *cartridge* in my right knee just before football season started.

Chikungunya fever is a *misquote* borne disease, meaning a human gets infected when bit by an infected *misquote* though the disease is not fatal.

He is the chief of pediatric hematology and oncology at *Mr.* Sinai Medical Center in New York.

I was helping the other allied health student change the garments and *appendages* of an elderly lady named Ruth.

The pain usually *deceases* with rest.

As I see it, hypnosis can be used as a successful *toot* for therapy.

These steps in CPR should be repeated until the victim has been *revised*.

His worst accident, he told me, was being on his dirt bike and taking a *shape conner*.

[article title on mixed parentage miscopied as] "Children of Mixed *Percentage*"

The law claims that we all are equal, but in fact we are sometimes judged because of our *shin* color.

The *Untied* States is very accepting of deformed and mental people.

According to the Bible, the truth of Jesus Christ will be *reviled* to Jews when the end of the world is near.

Evolutionary theories conflict with people who *interrupt* the bible literally.

Zen is the religious belief of the *boodiest*.

Just because Elton John and his partner are gay doesn't mean in any way that they are bad parents. They have the same amount of potential in becoming great *neutering* parents as straight couples do.

The hippie's outfit is then completed with leather *scandals* that have almost come apart.

There were several elderly people dressed like teeny-*boopers*.

Those too old to drive must get their licenses *revolted* by the state.

When she insulted me, that was the last *draw*.

Since no cars are available on the island, most people rent *mope heads* to ride around on.

This proposal has the support of various federal, state, and local *lawnmakers*.

Next, when he talks, *glaze* into his eyes.

Terry doesn't take time to think before acting.   He represents the typical *bronze* and no brain.

I started clowning around and trying to stand on my *heads* on the front of the boat.

This frustrating situation *decomposed* me because now I would be considered an irresponsible babysitter.

As we faced each other for karate sparring, we began to look for *venerable* body openings.

The U.S. now makes use of *tactful* cruise missiles.

When I forgot my gas mask, besides being choked by the gas, I had to take a lot of *ribbon* from the men.

I find myself enjoying things more with a girl who strongly believes in pre-*material* sex.

Neither do I agree with the argument that early marriage is protection against *premartial* sex relations.

Women in western culture are fiercely independent now, as many protests and marches will no *drought* tell you.

Because of the threat of skin cancer, we should all guard against *ultraviolent* rays.

Slow down your backswing and continue to *consecrate* by looking at the ball.

On the first day of class Mr. Ross showed us a slide *shoe* of his life.

There are some forms of life that exist but can't be seen by the *negative* eye.

He was the *valid victorian* of his senior class.

Avoid phrases that lay the blame on the other person. Instead of saying that he has it all wrong, try words that express your point of view in an *objectional* way.

By eliminating eight o'clock classes, students will have more time to prepare themselves for class and teachers can talk to a *tentative* class.

[Title of a how-to art essay] Finger *Pants*

This goal was *meat* in my essay "It's Too Hot."

My *writhing* in my essay "It's Too Hot" demonstrated rhetoric very well.

Later on in the article you learn that the man had donated money to Obama's *camping*.

In our research papers we had to *blind* our work with scholarly evidence.

The letter to my best friend was more personal and had *slain* words in it.

Bubble maps allow you to have something to go off of as you are in the *mist* of writing your paper.

My grammar use has *improvement* since the beginning of the semester.

A Word document does have a system of checking for grammatical errors, but it is not *full* proof.

In English 101, I have been taught how to write a perfect essay or come close to perfect essay. Over the course of this semester I have *wrote* three papers.

My content is fairly good, but my *dramatical* errors hurt my grade.

Classroom Comedy: Student Slips & Quips

(Collected from freshman essays)

Errors That Are Almost Right, Maybe Even *Should* Be Right

One negative aspect of a credit card is that it is too easy to abuse. It gives one free *excess* to credit.

Alicia wants to stay in Little Rock and work, but her boyfriend wants to move to Memphis after *marring* her.

From that point on in my lifetime, I have *tired* to listen to my elders.

I had three seconds for one last shot, but I lost the ball out of *bounce.*

Children are often *razed* by themselves.

Absence does not make the heart grow *founder.*

One girl stuck her hand through a window *pain.*

An individual should be cautious when viewing TV ads and not believe all that he sees. Therefore he should be very *weary* while watching the commercials.

When Dr. Warrington removed the gauze, I was praying I would not have any *scares.*

Although currently the United States Armed Forces are recruiting many men and women, some may argue that the country should implement a *constriction*.

The whole way out to the Cumberland bluffs I was bragging on how great I was at *repelling*.

I make sure I am always available when we have get-to-*gathers*.

My audience is next year's *on*coming freshmen.

In my faith there are rules for what can be considered appropriate in attire. It can be anything from a modest-length skirt to a neckline that is not too *reveling*.

After a few too many beers, I made the mistake of asking her to go watch the submarine races. She said she would love to go, so we *hoped* in my car.

More minority babies than minority families arc available for adoption. Some may think this is not *ethnical*, but a family that cares and loves a child is better than no family at all.

A study shows that educable mentally retarded students are usually *excepted* by other children as consistently as normal children.

Mondale uses the commercial to make Reagan look like some sort of war *mongrel*.

White states, "The Supreme Court justices ruled in 1879 that the free exercise clause of the First Amendment did not protect the Mormon practice of polygamy." Of course the *morons* who do practice polygamy would disagree and so would I.

Logic Problems and Word Misunderstandings

John Wilkes Booth escaped that night after his fatal leap to the stage.

Booth did in fact die sometime after the assassination and was then chased and killed by federal officers.

Mario Lanza once enjoyed a 23-egg omelet for breakfast. He died of a heart attack at 38, after which he dropped, on at least one occasion, 100 of his 270 pounds.

A long time ago, around 2000 B.C., people thought of Christmas as a time to celebrate the day on which Christ was born.

The drive from here to Charlotte is about two and a half hours by plane. From Charlotte she then takes a train to California, which takes six hours by plane.

Though I cannot say for certain, I'm sure I wouldn't be the same person I am today if I hadn't traveled.

A boy in a family of all girls shows more dominance and confidence.

My strength as a writer is that I can put words in ideas.

The easiest and most common trick for the elephant to learn is riding people.

The people who have told me of such dreams have been both male and female.

The clinic has been successful in lowering the number of unwanted pregnancies and in diagnosing other sexually transmitted diseases.

It was discovered by Dr. Joan Bauram and Dr. Robert Kolodny that only 12 percent of non-female pot smokers had defective menstrual cycles.

Most people feel lucky to just be living under a house with clothing and food.

Possibly Risqué Errors

Your back should be straight with the muscles in the neck and shoulders relaxed for an enjoyable jog. The head should be in a normal erotic position.

It is possible that high blood pressure can be lowered by being erect.

And let's not forget dating. You always meet guys you like to date, but how do you fit them in?

For the perfect kiss, I like to put my arms around the guy's neck and let him put his arms around my waste.

No one has business being bored unless they sin in their room all day.

Men, in fact, do the craziest things when their emotions are propelled into a woman.

Historical and Biblical examples of homosexual relationships indicate that homosexuality has penetrated the fortress of opponents of gay marriage.

I was ready to bat, so I took my usual hitting stance slightly crotched.

Kelly really got around. I mean she did not care whom it was with. One night she even made it with four different boys. This girl did not mess around.

By now the roads were completely frozen over and I was overjoyed. Spinning out and sliding my tail end around was very exciting to me.

Col. Hackworth believes male bondage is what makes military units work together.

Tied to the front bumper of his jeep, he had a wench.

In another scene of this ad, we see a lady washing her clothes in a laundromat. Then a man shows up and tries to get her tied, and she gets violent with him.

Old-fashioned, rigid doctors firmly believed that sex doesn't matter when a person reaches old age.

Venereal disease is becoming a problem all over the U.S. because health officials can't do it by themselves.

My essay's purpose is to warn my audience about the dangers of cutting corners and the humiliating reproductions that could follow.

If the wreck brings harm to you, you have to go to the hospital to get yourself fixed.

As I recall, I was in my dad's office going through his drawers when I found a most curious instrument that I had never seen before.

Missing Words

There don't have to be a lot of people present for you to screw and get an interesting nickname.
[screw *up*]

Driving your nuts is an easy yet fun activity.
[Driving your *teacher* nuts]

[Dear students: Thank you for driving me nuts for 31 years. It was a privilege and a lot of fun.]

Lit-Errata

For 31 years as a college literature teacher, I collected student gaffes that I thought were worth saving. I invite you to judge my teaching ability based on my students' grasp of the material. The errors come from exams and essays and are roughly arranged by literary chronology, beginning with world and British literature and then moving to American.

Oedipus was *dumbed* from birth.

Oedipus realizes that he was the one that killed his own father and married his *brother*.

When Jocasta finishes the story, Oedipus is *aroused* a little bit more than before.

Oedipus was a disgrace by being a murderer and being a *penetrator* of incest.

The first stage of Beowulf's life occurred when he was young. The next stage of Beowulf's life was when he was older.

In *Beowulf* the most important relationship was between a warrior and his lord. It was one of *neutral* trust and respect. The heroes in this work set out on *amos* adventure.

Beowulf was going to slay the beast with his *bear* hands.

Hamlet displays *fragrant* disrespect towards his mother the queen.

This quotation is a *syllabus* spoken at the end of the play. [soliloquy]

In "To His Coy Mistress" the persona wishes that if he had all the time he would stare into her eyes and her body.

Torvald merely looks at Nora as a doll which *turns* tricks to earn her stay.

In the essay "The Diamond Necklace" the *pearl* necklace symbolizes the meaning of the story.

Proust simply dipped a petite *mandolin* in his tea and was automatically taken back to a time in his childhood.

Even though the athlete in "To an Athlete Dying Young" is younger, he beat many of his opponents to death who were much older.

American literature was started in 1607 and ended in 1865.

Initiation, in my opinion, is a trial to see if you can make it through whatever circumstances necessary to reach a *pacific* goal.

Another term for sexual symbolism is *Fraudian* symbolism.

John Winthrop looked for *embalms* of the Bible everywhere.

A distinction can be made between Anne Bradstreet's private and *pubic* poetry.

This quotation is by Anne Bradstreet in "A Letter to Her Husband, Absent upon *Pubic* Employment."

In the line "Return, return sweet Sol, from Capricorn," Bradstreet is asking her dead husband to return to her. Sol is her husband's name.

What Thomas Morton gradually leads up to through this is an illustration of how ridiculous the Separatists are in their extremities.

Jonathan Edwards tries to *pervert* people to the church.

Washington Irving Americanized German *forktales*.

The headless horseman is a *fragment* of the people's imagination.

William Cullen Bryant in "To a Waterfowl" speaks of the waterfowl who flies alone, and he said we should follow in its footsteps.

Both in "Ulalume" and "The Raven" Poe uses the central theme of the death of a beautiful woman. The women in these two poems are past lovers.

Poe says that the most poetical topic in the world is the beauty of a deceased woman. [actually, the death of a beautiful woman]

Poe felt that you had to have a climax before you could write a poem.

Roderick Usher has a *spilt* personality.

Roderick tries to *enter* his still-living sister in a vault.

In "Masque of the Red Death" for the ones left outside who are infected with the plague, there is not *anecdote.*

"Young Goodman Brown" was written by Nathaniel *Hearthrone.*

Young Goodman Brown put the good people in the town on a *pedalstool.*

Robin in "My Kinsman Major Molineux" had the reputation of a *screwd* youth.

Hawthorne uses the ironic *epitaph* of "shrewd youth."

In Holmes' "The Chambered Nautilus," there is an idea of getting closer to heaven. The creature builds up his home, closer to God, and leaves his old behind.

The author of "Nature" is *Robert Waldolf* Emerson.

Thoreau's going to jail did not change anything; it was only a fruitless *jester.*

Whitman celebrates his existence in "Song of Myself." Through the use of grass as a symbol, he exposes himself to us.

Emily Dickinson used these images of death a lot in her poetry; and because of that she is one of the *transistors* from 19th century poetry to modern. Another *transistor* was Walt Whitman.

Stephanie Clinkscales said Emily Dickinson has eccentric *capitalism.*

In "Because I Could Not Stop for Death," the persona is being driven away very slowly and calmly in a *hertz*.

Billy Budd has been pressed into serving in the *navel* forces.

[miscopied title in endnote]: *12th Century Interpretations of* <u>*Huckleberry Finn*</u>

Huck travels the river with the King and the *Duck*.

Jim helped the doctor in treating Tom's gunshot *womb*.

Not many people in the world would like to read a *dole* essay about advice to youth. Twain's form of writing was always *corky* and unique to me.

In "Stopping by Woods on a Snowy Evening," Robert Frost used symbolism to convey the *underlining* meaning of his poem.

"Stopping by Woods on a Snowy Evening" was written by *Jack* Frost.

The part of man that once identified with nature *protrudes* as the persona observes the scenery.

"After Apple-Picking" should help people not to think so badly of death and dying, because going to *heave* will be the best life they will ever know.

Prufrock displays the *wound* fantasy. He desires to go back to his mother's *wound* where he will be protected from the world.

Prufrock has a womb *fallacy*.

"Do I dare / Disturb the Universe?" Here we see that the entire poem is about a question that would *electricute* everyone.

This line tells how Prufrock feels he's treated. He feels like he's the laughing *duck* at every party.

In *Cat on a Hot Tin Roof* Maggie hinted that she was devious and *kniving* at times, like a cat.

First off, Big Daddy is on the *blink* of dying.

The combination Hi-*five*, liquor cabinet, and TV stand symbolize all the ways that Brick tries to escape reality.

While Brick and Margaret are fighting about Brick's possibly homosexual relationship with Spencer, he tells her he doesn't love her either. [actual name = Skipper. Spencer is *my* name.]

In this passage Eudora Welty uses a *pond* (a word with two meanings).

Miss Emily had a crayon portrait of her father on a tarnished gilt easel. *Guilt* is a type of plating that was popular many years back.

Emily really likes Homer because she buys him a *toilet*, but he may not be happy with her.

This strange behavior that Miss *Evilly* displays is very mysterious and builds suspense.

The term for the perversion that Miss Emily practices is "narcalepsy." [necrophilia]

In *Ellen Foster*, Ellen finally finds a good friend (Starletta) but is most likely going to be *ostrichised* for it.

In *The Glass Menagerie* Amanda gets on to Tom for bringing an engaged gentleman caller to the house to *accomplish* his sister.

In *A Gathering of Old Men* the moral growth of the community, not just Charlie, is shown when the fight erupts amongst the old black man and Luke Will's *posy*. [posse]

The characters describe Fix Boutan as a ruthless leader of a *viscous* mob.

[And finally, with a look to the far, far, far future:]

There are several differences between *1900th* century and modern poets.

About the Author

Bill Spencer's humor writing has been published by *Funny Times*, *Narrative* magazine, *Reader's Digest*, *The Sun*, *The Inconsequential*, *Clever* magazine, *Defenestration*, *HumorOutcasts.com*, *The Short Humour Site*, *Hobo Pancakes*, and *Nuthouse*. He has also published scholarly articles on the novels of Cormac McCarthy, has written more than 140 comic skits performed at the Wildacres Writers Workshop, and has co-authored an unproduced screenplay entitled "Angel Pays a Visit." He taught English for thirty-one years, twenty-five of them at Delta State University and six at Western Carolina University. He lives in a cabin in the mountains of North Carolina with his wife, artist-poet Carolyn Elkins.

www.ingramcontent.com/pod-product-compliance
Lightning Source LLC
LaVergne TN
LVHW051505080426
835509LV00017B/1931